AF446522

Discovering Biblical Treasures

UNDERSTANDING KOHELET (ECCLESIASTES)

A commentary using Ancient Bible Study Methods

Michael Harvey Koplitz

This edition copyright ©2020. Michael H. Koplitz.

All rights reserved. No part of this publication may be reproduced or transmitted in any form or by any means without the permission of the publisher.

All Scripture quotations, unless otherwise noted, are taken from the New American Standard Bible®, Copyright © 1960, 1962, 1963, 1968, 1971, 1972, 1973, 1975, 1977, 1995 by the Lockman Foundation. Used by permission. (www.Lockman.org)

The NASB uses italic to indicate words that have been added for clarification. Citations are shown with large capital letters.

Published by Michael H. Koplitz

Acknowledgment

This work could not have been accomplished without Dr. Anne Davis, who taught me Ancient (Hebraic) Bible study methods, and my two study partners, Rev. Dr. Robert Cook, and Pastor Sandra Koplitz. We know that the journey has just started and will last a lifetime. The discovery of the depths of God's Word is waiting for us to find.

Table of Contents

Introduction

While I was attending Seminary earning my M. Div. degree, I started to question what the instructors and reference books were saying about the Scriptures. One of the ideas being offered then was that the Bible was full of errors and not factual. I found that attitude disturbing for Seminary instructors to be teaching. After all, the Seminary experience is to train pastors to go out into God's world and preach the Bible. How can you preach the Bible if you believe what these instructors are teaching? The methods that were being taught to examine the Bible just seemed inaccurate to me.

After graduating from Seminary, I spent much time reading different views about the Bible. I eventually read the Zohar. This collection of Midrashim is considered the secret work of the Torah, according to Kabbalists. Also, I learned quite a bit about Messianic Judaism. Their view of the Bible is quite different from the Seminary view.

I decided that the biblical interpretation that was being taught in Seminary was not the biblical interpretation the people heard when Jesus Christ (whose Hebraic name is Yeshua) preached. I went on a quest to learn what the people of Yeshua's day thought about Scripture, and what they thought when the Scriptures were read. This quest led me to Dr. Anne Davis and The Bible Learning University. Dr. Davis was in search of the same thing I was searching for. She had made many discoveries that helped me in my quest. I earned the Ph. D. degree from The Bible Learning University in Hebraic Studies in Christianity concentrating on ancient Bible Studies methods.

Finally, I found someone who believed that the church had placed almost 1900 years of theological ideas about the Scriptures and in many places possibly distorting its original meaning. What is also essential to hear is that the basic tenants of Yeshua as God's Messiah, my Lord and Savior are in the Bible. My faith in Yeshua is stronger now that I have learned from Dr. Davis how to study the Scriptures in the same manner that the people did in Yeshua's day.

I have included an article that describes the differences between Greek learning methods and Hebraic learning methods. Please do not skip this chapter unless you are familiar with ancient Bible study methods because if you do, then the analysis and commentary that follows may become difficult for you to understand.

Our God is vast and infinite, and so is His Word. May God bless you in your discovery of what God's Word is about.

The Greek name for this biblical book is Ecclesiastes. The Aramaic name for the book is Kohlat. The Hebrew name is Kohelet. Ecclesiastes in English means "the one who assembled." Kohlat and Kohelet in English mean "the voice, the words," that is "the preaching." The first verse of the book tells the reader that the author of the book is King Solomon, son of David.

King Solomon was a wealthy king. What Solomon discovered was that life is vanity. One is born into the world naked, with nothing, and leaves this world bare, with nothing. The book contains wise sayings, axioms, cautions, and instructions. This book is considered a wisdom book in the Tanakh.[1]

---

[1] Rocco A. Errico and George M. Lamsa, *Aramaic Light on Ezra through the Song of Solomon* (Smyma, GA: Noohra Foundation, 2010).

The main differences between the Greek method and the Hebraic method of teaching

Once a student becomes aware of these two teaching styles, the student will be able to determine if the class attended or if a book read, whether the teaching method is either a Greek or Hebraic method. In the Greek manner, the instructor is always right because of advanced knowledge. In the college situation, it is because the professor has his/her Ph.D. in some area of study, so one assumes that he or she knows everything about the topic. For example, Rodney Dangerfield played the role of a middle-aged man going to college. His English midterm was to write about Kurt Vonnegut Jr. Since he did not understand any of Vonnegut's books he hired Vonnegut himself to write the midterm. When he received the paper from the English Professor told Dangerfield that whoever wrote the paper knew nothing about Vonnegut. The professor's words are an example of the Greek method of teaching. Did the Ph.D. English professor think that she knew more about Vonnegut's writings than Vonnegut did? [2]

In the Greek teaching method, the professor or the instructor claims to be the authority. If one attends a Bible study class and the class leader says, "I will teach you the only way to understand this biblical book," you may want to consider the implications. This method is standard since most Seminaries and Bible colleges teach a Greek mode of learning, which is the same method the church has been utilizing for centuries.

---

[2] *Back to School*. Performed by Rodney Dangerfield. Hollywood: CA: Paper Clip Productions, 1986. DVD.

Hebraic teaching methods are different. The teacher wants the students to challenge what they hear. It is through questioning that a student can learn. Also, the teacher wants his/her students to excel to a point where the student becomes the teacher.

If two rabbis come together to discuss a passage of Scripture, the result will be at least ten different opinions. All points of view are acceptable if each is supported by biblical evidence. It is permissible and encouraged that students develop many ideas. There is a depth to God's Word, and God wants us to find all His messages contained in the Scripture.

Seeking out the meaning of the Scriptures beyond the literal meaning is essential to understand God's Word fully.[3] The Greek method of learning the Scriptures has prevailed over the centuries. One problem is that only the literal interpretation of Scripture was often viewed as valid, as prompted by Martin Luther's "sola literalis" meaning that just the literal translation of Scripture was accurate. The Fundamentalist movements of today base their beliefs on the literal interpretation of the Scripture. Therefore, they do not believe that God placed more profound, hidden, or secret meanings in the Word.

The students of the Scriptures who learn through Hebraic training and understanding have drawn a different conclusion. The Hebrew language itself leads to different possible interpretations because of the construction of the language. The Hebraic method of Bible study opens avenues of thought about God's revelations in the Scripture never considered. Not all questions about the Scripture studied will have an

---

[3] Davis, Anne Kimball. *The Synoptic Gospels*. MP3. Albuquerque: NM: BibleInteract, 2012.

immediate answer. If so, it becomes the responsibility of the learners to uncover the meaning. Also, remember that many opinions about the meaning of Scripture are also acceptable.

Methodology

The methodology employed is to use First Century Scripture study methods integrated with the customs and culture of Yeshua's day to examine the Hebrew and Christian Scriptures, thus gathering a more in-depth understanding by learning the Scriptures in the way the people of Yeshua's day did.

I have titled the methodology of analyzing a passage of Scripture in a Hebraic manner the "Process of Discovery." The author developed this methodology which brings together the various areas of linguistic and cultural understanding. There are several sections to the process, and not all the parts apply to every passage of Scripture. The overall result of developing this process is to give the reader a framework for studying the word in more depth.

The "Process of Discovery" starts with a Scripture passage. An examination of the linguistic structure of the passage is next. The linguistic structure includes parallelism, chiastic structures, and repetition. Formatting the passage in its linguistic form allows the reader to be able to visualize what the first century CE listener was hearing. Their corresponding sections label the chiasms, for example, A, B, C, B', A.' Not all passages of the Scriptures have a poetic form.

The next step is to "question the narrative." The questioning the narrative process assuming the reader knows nothing about the passage. Therefore, the questions go from the simple to the complex. The next task is to identify any linguistic patterns. Linguistic patterns include, but are not limited to irony, simile, metaphor, symbolism, idioms, hyperbole, figurative language, personification, and allegory.

A review of any translation inconsistencies discovered between the English NAU version and either the Hebrew or Greek versions is done. There are times when a Hebrew or Greek word is translated in more than one way. Inconsistencies also can be created by the translation committee, which may have decided to use traditional language instead of the actual translation. The decision of the translation committee is in the Preface or Introduction to the Bible. Perhaps some of the inconsistencies were intentionally added to convey some deeper meaning. An examination for every discrepancy is done.

The passage is analyzed for any echoes of the Hebrew Scriptures in the Christian Scriptures. Using a passage from the Hebrew Scriptures in the Christian Scriptures, an echo occurs.[4] Also, echoes are found when Torah (Genesis through Deuteronomy) passages , in other Hebrew Bible books. Cross-references in the Scripture are references from one verse to another verse which can assist the reader in understanding the verse.

The names of persons mentioned in the passage are listed. Many of the Hebrew names have meaning and may be associated with places or actions. Jewish parents used to name their children based on what they felt God had in store for their child. An example of this is Abraham whose original name was Abram and was changed to mean eternal father (God changed Abram's name to Abraham indicating a function he was to perform). When the Hebrew Bible gives names, many of the occurrences mean

---

[4] Mitzvot are the 613 commandments found in the Torah that please God. There are positive and negative commandments. The list was first development by Maimonides. The full list can be found at: ttp://www.jewfaq.org/613.htm.

something unique. The same importance can occur for the names of places. The time it takes to travel between locations can supply insight into the event.

Key phrases are identified in verses when they are essential to an understanding of that passage. There are no rules for selecting the keywords. Searching for other occurrences of the keywords in Scripture in a concordance is necessary to understand the word's usage; this must be done in either Hebrew or Greek, not in English. A classic Hebraic approach is to find the usage of a word in the Scripture by finding other verses that contain the word. The usage of a word, in its original language, is discovered by searching the Scripture in the language of the word. Verses that contain the word are identified, and a pattern for the usage of the word discovered. Each verse is examined to see what the usage of the word is which, may reveal a model for the word's usage. For Hebrew words the first usage of the word in the Scripture, primarily if used in the Torah, is essential. For the Greek words, the Christian Scriptures are used to determine the word usage in the Scripture. Sometimes finding the equivalent Greek word in the Septuagint then analyzing its usage in Hebrew can be very helpful.

The Rules of Hillel are used when applicable. Hillel was a Torah scholar who lived shortly before Yeshua's day. Hillel developed several rules for Torah students to interpret the Scriptures which refer to halachic Midrash. In several cases, these rules are helpful in the analysis of the Scripture.

The cultural implications from the period of the writing are done after the linguistic analysis is completed. The culture is crucial because it is not explicitly referenced in the biblical narratives as indicated earlier.

From the linguistic analysis and the cultural understanding, it is possible to obtain a deeper meaning of the Scripture beyond the literal meaning of the plain text. That is what the listeners of Yeshua's time were doing. They put the linguistics and the culture together without even having to contemplate it. They simply did it.

The analysis will lead to a set of findings explaining what the passage meant in Yeshua's day. Most of the time the Hebraic analysis leads to the desire for more in-depth analysis to fully understand what Yeshua was talking about or what was happening to Him. Whatever the result, a new more in-depth understanding of the Scripture is obtained.

The components of the Process of Discovery are:

Language

  Process of Discovery

    Linguistics Section

      Linguistic Structure

      Discussion

      Questioning the Passage

      Verse Comparison of citations or proof text

      Translation Inconsistencies

      Biblical Personalities

      Biblical Locations

      Phrase Study

      Scripture cross-references

      Linguistic Echoes

Only the areas needed for each chapter is included.

Chapter One

Language

New American Standard 1995	Hebrew
[1] The words of the Preacher, the son of David, king in Jerusalem.	דִּבְרֵי֙ קֹהֶ֣לֶת בֶּן־דָּוִ֔ד מֶ֖לֶךְ בִּירוּשָׁלָֽ͏ִם׃ [2] הֲבֵ֤ל
[2] "Vanity of vanities," says the Preacher, "Vanity of vanities! All is vanity."	הֲבָלִים֙ אָמַ֣ר קֹהֶ֔לֶת הֲבֵ֥ל הֲבָלִ֖ים הַכֹּ֥ל הָֽבֶל׃ [3] מַה־יִּתְר֖וֹן לָֽאָדָ֑ם בְּכָל־עֲמָל֔וֹ שֶֽׁיַּעֲמֹ֖ל תַּ֥חַת הַשָּֽׁמֶשׁ׃
[3] What advantage does man have in all his work Which he does under the sun?	[4] דּ֤וֹר הֹלֵךְ֙ וְד֣וֹר בָּ֔א וְהָאָ֖רֶץ לְעוֹלָ֥ם עֹמָֽדֶת׃
[4] A generation goes and a generation comes, But the earth remains forever.	[5] וְזָרַ֥ח הַשֶּׁ֖מֶשׁ וּבָ֣א הַשָּׁ֑מֶשׁ וְאֶ֨ל־מְקוֹמ֔וֹ שׁוֹאֵ֛ף זוֹרֵ֥חַ ה֖וּא שָֽׁם׃
[5] Also, the sun rises and the sun sets; And hastening to its place it rises there *again*.	[6] הוֹלֵךְ֙ אֶל־דָּר֔וֹם וְסוֹבֵ֖ב אֶל־צָפ֑וֹן סוֹבֵ֤ב ׀ סֹבֵב֙ הוֹלֵ֣ךְ הָר֔וּחַ וְעַל־סְבִיבֹתָ֖יו שָׁ֥ב הָרֽוּחַ׃
[6] Blowing toward the south, Then turning toward the north, The wind continues swirling along; And on its circular courses the wind returns.	[7] כָּל־הַנְּחָלִים֙ הֹלְכִ֣ים אֶל־הַיָּ֔ם וְהַיָּ֖ם אֵינֶ֣נּוּ מָלֵ֑א אֶל־מְק֗וֹם שֶׁ֤הַנְּחָלִים֙ הֹֽלְכִ֔ים שָׁ֛ם הֵ֥ם שָׁבִ֖ים לָלָֽכֶת׃
[7] All the rivers flow into the sea, Yet the sea is not full. To the place where the rivers flow, There they flow again.	[8] כָּל־הַדְּבָרִ֣ים יְגֵעִ֔ים לֹא־יוּכַ֥ל אִ֖ישׁ לְדַבֵּ֑ר לֹא־תִשְׂבַּ֥ע עַ֙יִן֙ לִרְא֔וֹת וְלֹא־תִמָּלֵ֥א אֹ֖זֶן מִשְּׁמֹֽעַ׃
[8] All things are wearisome; Man is not able to tell *it*. The eye is not satisfied with seeing, Nor is the ear filled with hearing.	[9] מַה־שֶּֽׁהָיָה֙ ה֣וּא שֶׁיִּהְיֶ֔ה וּמַה־שֶּׁנַּֽעֲשָׂ֔ה ה֖וּא שֶׁיֵּעָשֶׂ֑ה וְאֵ֥ין כָּל־חָדָ֖שׁ תַּ֥חַת הַשָּֽׁמֶשׁ׃
[9] That which has been is that which will be, And that which has been done is that which will be done. So there is nothing new under the sun.	[10] יֵ֥שׁ דָּבָ֛ר שֶׁיֹּאמַ֥ר רְאֵה־זֶ֖ה חָדָ֣שׁ ה֑וּא כְּבָר֙ הָיָ֣ה לְעֹֽלָמִ֔ים אֲשֶׁ֥ר הָיָ֖ה מִלְּפָנֵֽנוּ׃
[10] Is there anything of which one might say, "See this, it is new "? Already it has existed for ages Which were before us.	[11] אֵ֥ין זִכְר֖וֹן לָרִאשֹׁנִ֑ים וְגַ֨ם לָאַחֲרֹנִ֜ים שֶׁיִּהְי֗וּ לֹֽא־יִהְיֶ֤ה לָהֶם֙ זִכָּר֔וֹן עִ֥ם שֶׁיִּהְי֖וּ לָאַחֲרֹנָֽה׃ פ
[11] There is no remembrance of earlier things; And also of the later things which will occur, There will be for them no remembrance Among those who will come later *still*.	[12] אֲנִ֣י קֹהֶ֗לֶת הָיִ֥יתִי מֶ֛לֶךְ עַל־יִשְׂרָאֵ֖ל בִּירוּשָׁלָֽ͏ִם׃ [13] וְנָתַ֣תִּי אֶת־לִבִּ֗י לִדְר֤וֹשׁ וְלָתוּר֙ בַּֽחָכְמָ֔ה עַ֛ל כָּל־אֲשֶׁ֥ר נַעֲשָׂ֖ה תַּ֣חַת הַשָּׁמָ֑יִם ה֣וּא ׀ עִנְיַ֣ן רָ֗ע נָתַ֧ן אֱלֹהִ֛ים לִבְנֵ֥י הָאָדָ֖ם לַעֲנ֥וֹת בּֽוֹ׃ [14] רָאִ֙יתִי֙ אֶת־כָּל־הַֽמַּעֲשִׂ֔ים שֶֽׁנַּעֲשׂ֖וּ תַּ֣חַת הַשָּׁ֑מֶשׁ וְהִנֵּ֥ה הַכֹּ֛ל הֶ֖בֶל וּרְע֥וּת רֽוּחַ׃ [15] מְעֻוָּ֖ת לֹא־יוּכַ֣ל לִתְקֹ֑ן וְחֶסְר֖וֹן לֹא־יוּכַ֥ל לְהִמָּנֽוֹת׃ [16] דִּבַּ֨רְתִּי אֲנִ֤י עִם־לִבִּי֙ לֵאמֹ֔ר אֲנִ֗י הִנֵּ֨ה הִגְדַּ֤לְתִּי וְהוֹסַ֙פְתִּי֙ חָכְמָ֔ה עַ֥ל כָּל־אֲשֶׁר־הָיָ֥ה

12 I, the Preacher, have been king over Israel in Jerusalem.

13 And I set my mind to seek and explore by wisdom concerning all that has been done under heaven. *It* is a grievous task *which* God has given to the sons of men to be afflicted with.

14 I have seen all the works which have been done under the sun, and behold, all is vanity and striving after wind.

15 What is crooked cannot be straightened and what is lacking cannot be counted.

16 I said to myself, "Behold, I have magnified and increased wisdom more than all who were over Jerusalem before me; and my mind has observed a wealth of wisdom and knowledge."

17 And I set my mind to know wisdom and to know madness and folly; I realized that this also is striving after wind.

18 Because in much wisdom there is much grief, and increasing knowledge *results in* increasing pain.

לְפָנַי עַל־יְרוּשָׁלָ͏ִם וְלִבִּי רָאָה הַרְבֵּה חׇכְמָה וָדָעַת:

17 וָאֶתְּנָה לִבִּי לָדַעַת חׇכְמָה וְדַעַת הוֹלֵלוֹת וְשִׂכְלוּת יָדַעְתִּי שֶׁגַּם־זֶה הוּא רַעְיוֹן רוּחַ:

18 כִּי בְּרֹב חׇכְמָה רׇב־כָּעַס וְיוֹסִיף דַּעַת יוֹסִיף מַכְאוֹב:

Process of Discovery

Linguistics Section

Linguistic Structure

[1] The words of the Preacher, the son of David, king in Jerusalem.

A [2] "Vanity of vanities," says the Preacher, "Vanity of vanities! All is vanity." [3] What advantage does man have in all his work Which he does under the sun?

> **B** [4] A generation goes and a generation comes, But the earth remains forever. [5] Also, the sun rises and the sun sets; And hastening to its place it rises there *again*. [6] Blowing toward the south, Then turning toward the north, The wind continues swirling along; And on its circular courses the wind returns. [7] All the rivers flow into the sea, Yet the sea is not full. To the place where the rivers flow, There they flow again. [8] All things are wearisome; Man is not able to tell *it*. The eye is not satisfied with seeing, Nor is the ear filled with hearing.

A' [9] That which has been is that which will be, And that which has been done is that which will be done. So there is nothing new under the sun.

> **B'** [10] Is there anything of which one might say, "See this, it is new "? Already it has existed for ages Which were before us. [11] There is no remembrance of earlier things; And also of the later things which will occur, There will be for them no remembrance Among those who will come later *still*.

A [12] I, the Preacher, have been king over Israel in Jerusalem. [13] And I set my mind to seek and explore by wisdom concerning all that has been done under heaven. *It* is a grievous task *which* God has given to the sons of men to be afflicted with. [14] I have seen all the works which have been done under the sun, and behold, all is vanity and striving after wind.

> **B** [15] What is crooked cannot be straightened and what is lacking cannot be counted.

A' [16] I said to myself, "Behold, I have magnified and increased wisdom more than all who were over Jerusalem before me; and my mind has observed a wealth of wisdom and knowledge."[17] And I set my mind to know wisdom and to know madness and folly; I realized that this also is striving after wind.

B' [18] Because in much wisdom there is much grief, and increasing knowledge *results in* increasing pain.

Discussion

King Solomon was given the divine gift of wisdom and understanding. In 1 Kings 3:4-14, the narrative of the LORD's visit to King Solomon occurred. In this visit, Solomon asked for wisdom and knowledge, which the LORD granted to him. During his reign, the Queen of Sheba heard about King Solomon's wisdom and came to Jerusalem to prove his wisdom against her dark sayings. Solomon's wisdom led him to the understanding that materialism was not the goal of life.

Questioning the Passage

1. Why was Solomon called a preacher? (v. 1)

    In 1 Kings 8:1, Solomon spoke his words of wisdom found in this book in public. Midrash says that people flocked to hear the words of the King. A person who spoke in public and had an audience was called a preacher.[5]

2. What did Solomon mean in verse two?

    According to the Targum of Kohelet, Solomon had a vision through the Shekinah that his kingdom was going to be divided between Rehoboam, his

---

[5] Nosson Scherman and Meir Zlotowitz, *The Book of Megillos: the Five Megillos: a New Translation with Overviews and Annotations Anthologized from the Classical Commentators* (Brooklyn, NY: Mesorah Publications, 1986).

son and Jeroboam the son of Nabat and that in time the Temple that he built for the LORD was going to be destroyed. Solomon proclaimed that the earthly work that he and David did for the LORD was for the vanity of the people and not for the LORD.[6]

If the Temple was for the LORD alone and not for the people, then how could it possibly be destroyed? This attitude can be applied to the building of fancy synagogues and churches throughout the centuries. Did the LORD ask for these magnificent buildings, or did the vanity of the people call for them?

When Notre Dame burned in 2019, what was the reaction of the catholic church? They were concerned about the history and artifacts contained in the building. Was the concern vanity? Does Notre Dame, and other religious buildings stand for the glory of the LORD or the beauty of the human-made institution, the church?

3. What does "a generation comes and goes" mean in verse four?
    The Targum states that King Solomon saw through the spirit of prophecy that a generation of righteous persons departs from this world because of the sins of the evil age of wicked ones who will come after them. This sentiment is also said in Isaiah 57:1.

    Is. 57:1 The righteous man perishes, and no man takes it to heart; And devout men are taken away, while no one understands. For the righteous man is taken away from evil.

---

[6] Martin McNamara et al., *The Aramaic Bible. the Targums: The Targum of Job, the Targum of Proverbs, the Targum of Qohelet*, 1991.

4. What are the references to the wind in verse six?

The Targum says that the directions of the wind to the south are dictated by the vernal equinox and the summer solstice. The winds turn to the north dictated by the autumnal equinox and the summer solstice.

5. What is the meaning of verse eight?

The Targum says that the prophets of the LORD could tell of future prophecy about other people, but they could not see their future. Since the prophets could not understand their future, no human can see what their future will bring.

6. What is the meaning of verse nine?

This verse is referring to eternal wisdom. For example, the Assyrians invented the wheel. Their civilization is long gone, but the knowledge of the wheel is used today to make automobiles, trucks, bicycles, and other inventions possible.[7] All areas of science and culture develop from the discoveries and inventions that proceeded them.

7. Who is coming later in verse eleven?

This reference is about the days of the Messiah.[8]

8. What does verse thirteen mean?

King Solomon said that he immersed himself in the materialism of the words. He studied philosophy and in his quest for material things, he

---

[7] Rocco A. Errico and George M. Lamsa, *Aramaic Light on Ezra through the Song of Solomon* (Smyrna, GA: Noohra Foundation, 2010).

[8] Martin McNamara et al., *The Aramaic Bible. the Targums: The Targum of Job, the Targum of Proverbs, the Targum of Qohelet*, 1991.

realized that the evil mentioned in the Torah refers to this obsessive quest for mundanity and riches with which man is always preoccupied. Solomon understood that humans need to seek a livelihood. However, livelihood and the pursuit of materialism must not consume the person.[9]

9. What does verse fifteen mean?

One view of this verse is that humans cannot change nature. The LORD created nature and set it in motion. Another aspect is that humans cannot create something new that was not already established by the LORD. A third view is that a human who was wicked in life cannot become righteous after death.

10. What does verse eighteen say?

The Targum states that when humans increase their sin and do not repent of the sin, it angers the LORD. Also, a person who gains wisdom but dies as a youth increases the heartache of his/her relatives.

---

[9] Nosson Scherman and Meir Zlotowitz, *The Book of Megillos: the Five Megillos: a New Translation with Overviews and Annotations Anthologized from the Classical Commentators* (Brooklyn, NY: Mesorah Publications, 1986).

Phrase Study

1. קֹהֶלֶת (qōhelet) speaker in an assembly, Qoheleth.[10] (v. 1) Another translation is "preacher." This book is equivalent to a sermon given by the King.

2. שֶׁיַּעֲמֹל תַּחַת הַשָּׁמֶשׁ (v. 3) This phrase is translated as "which he does under the sun." *Amel* should be translated as "toil" or "work," as it is translated in the first part of the sentence.

3. עָמֵל (ʿāmēl) II, toiling. (v. 3)

"The verb עָמַל is one of several Hebrew verbs for "labor, work, toil." Other major terms include עָבַד "to work, serve," and עָצָה "to make, do, work" (both of which see). עָמַל is used less often than those two verbs, and is employed often with the nuance of the drudgery of toil rather than the nobility of labor. Hebrew עָמַל is cognate to Arabic ʿamila "to labor," and to the Akkadian noun nīmēlu, that produced by work, "gain, possessions."

The root עָמַל relates to the dark side of labor, the grievous and unfulfilling aspect of work. A biblical view of labor based on this word alone would be defective, but this aspect of work should be included in a full induction. Thus Moses uses this term to describe the frustration and struggle of the worker in this ephemeral, transitory world (Ps 90:10). No wonder he cries out to the eternal God "and let thy beauty (eternal, lovely work) be upon us" (v. 17). The root in its several forms is used especially by Solomon in Eccl as he details the frustration, profitlessness,

---

[10] TWOT electronic version from Accordance Bible Software V. 13

and transitory (הֶבֶל) benefits of day-by-day labor; such is noted when that labor is not seen as service (even worship!) to God, but simply as work done "under the sun." For the man whose relationship to God is tenuous, there is no profit (יִתְרוֹן) from all his work (Eccl 1:3). Yet even in Eccl there are glimpses of a higher view of labor: "every one who eats and drinks and sees good in all his labor-it is the gift of God" (3:13; cf. 5:18–19 [H 17–18])."[11]

The work that this verse is referring to is the work that is done in the light of the day. A few women in a village may do some work in the evening, but overall work stops. During the evening hours between midnight and 3:00 AM, the Torah study was conducted in the home. The study of the Torah was and is considered a Mitzvah. The work during the day had to be done to survive. For example, the farmer would tend to his fields and the animals. Without food, people would not survive. That could be considered the dark side of labor because it does not benefit the soul but rather the flesh. The work done to study the Torah is pleasing to the LORD. The profit that King Solomon is referring to is the profit of knowing the LORD and living in a way that not only benefits the person but also pleases the LORD.

4. עָוַת (ʿāwat) *bend, make crooked, pervert."* (ASV, RSV similar with the former using such synonyms as "subvert" and "overthrow.") Used only in the intensive conjugations."[12] (v. 15)

---

[11] IBID.
[12] IBID.

Thoughts

The main idea Solomon is grasping at is the value of wisdom and its comparison to materialism. The collecting of material objects is necessary to survive, but when this act overshadows the studying of the Torah and the Words of the LORD, then it turns to evil. There are so many distractions that take people away from the study of the Bible. In today's churches, about five percent (and that is on the high side) of the people in the Sunday worship celebrations do any biblical study. Unfortunately, this problem is compounded because most churches do not have educated and trained teachers to lead biblical studies. Every believer in the LORD obligates themselves to study the Torah even if it has to be done by oneself. Proper wisdom from the LORD is obtained when following His Word.

Chapter Two

Language

New American Standard 1995	Hebrew
[1] I said to myself, "Come now, I will test you with pleasure. So enjoy yourself." And behold, it too was futility. [2] I said of laughter, "It is madness," and of pleasure, "What does it accomplish?" [3] I explored with my mind *how* to stimulate my body with wine while my mind was guiding *me* wisely, and how to take hold of folly, until I could see what good there is for the sons of men to do under heaven the few years of their lives. [4] I enlarged my works: I built houses for myself, I planted vineyards for myself; [5] I made gardens and parks for myself and I planted in them all kinds of fruit trees; [6] I made ponds of water for myself from which to irrigate a forest of growing trees. [7] I bought male and female slaves and I had homeborn slaves. Also I possessed flocks and herds larger than all who preceded me in Jerusalem. [8] Also, I collected for myself silver and gold and the treasure of kings and provinces. I provided for myself male and female singers and the pleasures of men-- many concubines. [9] Then I became great and increased more than all who preceded me in Jerusalem. My wisdom also stood by me. [10] All that my eyes desired I did not refuse them. I did not withhold my heart from any pleasure, for my heart was pleased because of all my labor and this was my reward for all my labor.	אָמַרְתִּי אֲנִי בְּלִבִּי לְכָה־נָּא אֲנַסְּכָה בְשִׂמְחָה וּרְאֵה בְטוֹב וְהִנֵּה גַם־הוּא הָבֶל: 2לִשְׂחוֹק אָמַרְתִּי מְהוֹלָל וּלְשִׂמְחָה מַה־זֹּה עֹשָׂה: 3 תַּרְתִּי בְלִבִּי לִמְשׁוֹךְ בַּיַּיִן אֶת־בְּשָׂרִי וְלִבִּי נֹהֵג בַּחָכְמָה וְלֶאֱחֹז בְּסִכְלוּת עַד אֲשֶׁר־אֶרְאֶה אֵי־זֶה טוֹב לִבְנֵי הָאָדָם אֲשֶׁר יַעֲשׂוּ תַּחַת הַשָּׁמַיִם מִסְפַּר יְמֵי חַיֵּיהֶם: 4 הִגְדַּלְתִּי מַעֲשָׂי בָּנִיתִי לִי בָּתִּים נָטַעְתִּי לִי כְּרָמִים: 5 עָשִׂיתִי לִי גַּנּוֹת וּפַרְדֵּסִים וְנָטַעְתִּי בָהֶם עֵץ כָּל־פֶּרִי: 6 עָשִׂיתִי לִי בְּרֵכוֹת מָיִם לְהַשְׁקוֹת מֵהֶם יַעַר צוֹמֵחַ עֵצִים: 7 קָנִיתִי עֲבָדִים וּשְׁפָחוֹת וּבְנֵי־בַיִת הָיָה לִי גַּם מִקְנֶה בָקָר וָצֹאן הַרְבֵּה הָיָה לִי מִכֹּל שֶׁהָיוּ לְפָנַי בִּירוּשָׁלָ͏ִם: 8 כָּנַסְתִּי לִי גַּם־כֶּסֶף וְזָהָב וּסְגֻלַּת מְלָכִים וְהַמְּדִינוֹת עָשִׂיתִי לִי שָׁרִים וְשָׁרוֹת וְתַעֲנוּגֹת בְּנֵי הָאָדָם שִׁדָּה וְשִׁדּוֹת: 9 וְגָדַלְתִּי וְהוֹסַפְתִּי מִכֹּל שֶׁהָיָה לְפָנַי בִּירוּשָׁלָ͏ִם אַף חָכְמָתִי עָמְדָה לִּי: 10 וְכֹל אֲשֶׁר שָׁאֲלוּ עֵינַי לֹא אָצַלְתִּי מֵהֶם לֹא־מָנַעְתִּי אֶת־לִבִּי מִכָּל־שִׂמְחָה כִּי־לִבִּי שָׂמֵחַ מִכָּל־עֲמָלִי וְזֶה־הָיָה חֶלְקִי מִכָּל־עֲמָלִי: 11 וּפָנִיתִי אֲנִי בְּכָל־מַעֲשַׂי שֶׁעָשׂוּ יָדַי וּבֶעָמָל שֶׁעָמַלְתִּי לַעֲשׂוֹת וְהִנֵּה הַכֹּל הֶבֶל וּרְעוּת רוּחַ וְאֵין יִתְרוֹן תַּחַת הַשָּׁמֶשׁ: 12 וּפָנִיתִי אֲנִי לִרְאוֹת חָכְמָה וְהוֹלֵלוֹת וְסִכְלוּת כִּי מֶה הָאָדָם שֶׁיָּבוֹא אַחֲרֵי הַמֶּלֶךְ אֵת אֲשֶׁר־כְּבָר עָשׂוּהוּ: 13 וְרָאִיתִי אָנִי שֶׁיֵּשׁ יִתְרוֹן לַחָכְמָה מִן־הַסִּכְלוּת כִּיתְרוֹן הָאוֹר מִן־הַחֹשֶׁךְ:

¹¹ Thus I considered all my activities which my hands had done and the labor which I had exerted, and behold all was vanity and striving after wind and there was no profit under the sun.

¹² So I turned to consider wisdom, madness and folly; for what *will* the man *do* who will come after the king *except* what has already been done?

¹³ And I saw that wisdom excels folly as light excels darkness.

¹⁴ The wise man's eyes are in his head, but the fool walks in darkness. And yet I know that one fate befalls them both.

¹⁵ Then I said to myself, "As is the fate of the fool, it will also befall me. Why then have I been extremely wise?" So I said to myself, "This too is vanity."

¹⁶ For there is no lasting remembrance of the wise man *as* with the fool, inasmuch as *in* the coming days all will be forgotten. And how the wise man and the fool alike die!

¹⁷ So I hated life, for the work which had been done under the sun was grievous to me; because everything is futility and striving after wind.

¹⁸ Thus I hated all the fruit of my labor for which I had labored under the sun, for I must leave it to the man who will come after me.

¹⁹ And who knows whether he will be a wise man or a fool? Yet he will have control over all the fruit of my labor for which I have labored by acting wisely under the sun. This too is vanity.

²⁰ Therefore I completely despaired of all the fruit of my labor for which I had labored under the sun.

²¹ When there is a man who has labored with wisdom, knowledge and skill, then

הֶחָכָם עֵינָיו בְּרֹאשׁוֹ וְהַכְּסִיל בַּחֹשֶׁךְ הוֹלֵךְ וְיָדַעְתִּי גַם־אָנִי שֶׁמִּקְרֶה אֶחָד יִקְרֶה אֶת־כֻּלָּם: ¹⁴

וְאָמַרְתִּי אֲנִי בְּלִבִּי כְּמִקְרֵה הַכְּסִיל גַּם־אֲנִי יִקְרֵנִי וְלָמָּה חָכַמְתִּי אֲנִי אָז יוֹתֵר וְדִבַּרְתִּי בְלִבִּי שֶׁגַּם־זֶה הָבֶל: ¹⁵

כִּי אֵין זִכְרוֹן לֶחָכָם עִם־הַכְּסִיל לְעוֹלָם בְּשֶׁכְּבָר הַיָּמִים הַבָּאִים הַכֹּל נִשְׁכָּח וְאֵיךְ יָמוּת הֶחָכָם עִם־הַכְּסִיל: ¹⁶

וְשָׂנֵאתִי אֶת־הַחַיִּים כִּי רַע עָלַי הַמַּעֲשֶׂה שֶׁנַּעֲשָׂה תַּחַת הַשָּׁמֶשׁ כִּי־הַכֹּל הֶבֶל וּרְעוּת רוּחַ: ¹⁷

וְשָׂנֵאתִי אֲנִי אֶת־כָּל־עֲמָלִי שֶׁאֲנִי עָמֵל תַּחַת הַשָּׁמֶשׁ שֶׁאַנִּיחֶנּוּ לְאָדָם שֶׁיִּהְיֶה אַחֲרָי: ¹⁸

וּמִי יוֹדֵעַ הֶחָכָם יִהְיֶה אוֹ סָכָל וְיִשְׁלַט בְּכָל־עֲמָלִי שֶׁעָמַלְתִּי וְשֶׁחָכַמְתִּי תַּחַת הַשָּׁמֶשׁ גַּם־זֶה הָבֶל: ¹⁹

וְסַבּוֹתִי אֲנִי לְיַאֵשׁ אֶת־לִבִּי עַל כָּל־הֶעָמָל שֶׁעָמַלְתִּי תַּחַת הַשָּׁמֶשׁ: ²⁰

כִּי־יֵשׁ אָדָם שֶׁעֲמָלוֹ בְּחָכְמָה וּבְדַעַת וּבְכִשְׁרוֹן וּלְאָדָם שֶׁלֹּא עָמַל־בּוֹ יִתְּנֶנּוּ חֶלְקוֹ גַּם־זֶה הֶבֶל וְרָעָה רַבָּה: ²¹

כִּי מֶה־הֹוֶה לָאָדָם בְּכָל־עֲמָלוֹ וּבְרַעְיוֹן לִבּוֹ שֶׁהוּא עָמֵל תַּחַת הַשָּׁמֶשׁ: ²²

כִּי כָל־יָמָיו מַכְאֹבִים וָכַעַס עִנְיָנוֹ גַּם־בַּלַּיְלָה לֹא־שָׁכַב לִבּוֹ גַּם־זֶה הֶבֶל הוּא: ²³

אֵין־טוֹב בָּאָדָם שֶׁיֹּאכַל וְשָׁתָה וְהֶרְאָה אֶת־נַפְשׁוֹ טוֹב בַּעֲמָלוֹ גַּם־זֹה רָאִיתִי אָנִי כִּי מִיַּד הָאֱלֹהִים הִיא: ²⁴

כִּי מִי יֹאכַל וּמִי יָחוּשׁ חוּץ מִמֶּנִּי: ²⁵

כִּי לְאָדָם שֶׁטּוֹב לְפָנָיו נָתַן חָכְמָה וְדַעַת וְשִׂמְחָה וְלַחוֹטֶא נָתַן עִנְיָן לֶאֱסוֹף וְלִכְנוֹס לָתֵת לְטוֹב לִפְנֵי הָאֱלֹהִים גַּם־זֶה הֶבֶל וּרְעוּת רוּחַ: ²⁶

he gives his legacy to one who has not labored with them. This too is vanity and a great evil.

²² For what does a man get in all his labor and in his striving with which he labors under the sun?

²³ Because all his days his task is painful and grievous; even at night his mind does not rest. This too is vanity.

²⁴ There is nothing better for a man *than* to eat and drink and tell himself that his labor is good. This also I have seen that it is from the hand of God.

²⁵ For who can eat and who can have enjoyment without Him?

²⁶ For to a person who is good in His sight He has given wisdom and knowledge and joy, while to the sinner He has given the task of gathering and collecting so that he may give to one who is good in God's sight. This too is vanity and striving after wind.

Process of Discovery

Linguistics Section

Linguistic Structure

A [1] I said to myself, "Come now, I will test you with pleasure. So enjoy yourself." And behold, it too was futility. [2] I said of laughter, "It is madness," and of pleasure, "What does it accomplish?"

> **B** [3] I explored with my mind *how* to stimulate my body with wine while my mind was guiding *me* wisely, and how to take hold of folly, until I could see what good there is for the sons of men to do under heaven the few years of their lives. [4] I enlarged my works: I built houses for myself, I planted vineyards for myself; [5] I made gardens and parks for myself and I planted in them all kinds of fruit trees; [6] I made ponds of water for myself from which to irrigate a forest of growing trees. [7] I bought male and female slaves and I had homeborn slaves. Also I possessed flocks and herds larger than all who preceded me in Jerusalem. [8] Also, I collected for myself silver and gold and the treasure of kings and provinces. I provided for myself male and female singers and the pleasures of men-- many concubines. [9] Then I became great and increased more than all who preceded me in Jerusalem. My wisdom also stood by me. [10] All that my eyes desired I did not refuse them. I did not withhold my heart from any pleasure, for my heart was pleased because of all my labor and this was my reward for all my labor.

A' [11] Thus I considered all my activities which my hands had done and the labor which I had exerted, and behold all was vanity and striving after wind and there was no profit under the sun.

A [12] So I turned to consider wisdom, madness and folly; for what *will* the man *do* who will come after the king *except* what has already been done? [13] And I saw that wisdom excels folly as light excels darkness. [14] The wise man's eyes are in his head, but the fool walks in darkness. And yet I know that one fate befalls them both. [15] Then I said to myself, "As is the fate of the fool, it will also befall me. Why then have I been extremely wise?" So I said to myself, "This too is vanity." [16] For there is no lasting remembrance of the wise man *as* with the fool, inasmuch as *in* the coming days all will be forgotten. And how the wise man and the fool alike die!

B [17] So I hated life, for the work which had been done under the sun was grievous to me; because everything is futility and striving after wind. [18] Thus I hated all the fruit of my labor for which I had labored under the sun, for I must leave it to the man who will come after me.

> **C** [19] And who knows whether he will be a wise man or a fool? Yet he will have control over all the fruit of my labor for which I have labored by acting wisely under the sun. This too is vanity.

B' [20] Therefore I completely despaired of all the fruit of my labor for which I had labored under the sun. [21] When there is a man who has labored with wisdom, knowledge and skill, then he gives his legacy to one who has not labored with them. This too is vanity and a great evil.

A' [22] For what does a man get in all his labor and in his striving with which he labors under the sun? [23] Because all his days his task is painful and grievous; even at night his mind does not rest. This too is vanity. [24] There is nothing better for a man *than* to eat and drink and tell himself that his labor is good. This also I have seen that it is from the hand of God. [25] For who can eat and who can have enjoyment without Him? [26] For to a person who is good in His sight He has given wisdom and knowledge and joy, while to the sinner He has given the task of gathering and collecting so that he may give to one who is good in God's sight. This too is vanity and striving after wind.

Discussion

The chapter consists of two chiasms. Each chiasm introduces a new topic for discussion.

Questioning the Passage

1. What is Solomon looking for in verse one?

   Solomon said that he had all the riches of the world at his disposal. However, he was not happy. Therefore, he believed that there was more to life than just material objects and sensual pleasures. He decided to go in search of these things.[13]

2. What does verse three say?

Solomon decided at first to further explore the lusts and habits of life. He attempted to grasp satisfaction from his previous pursuits. He also decided to drink heavily.[14]

3. What works did Solomon enlarge? (v. 4)

The Targum states that Solomon was referring to his ivory throne which is described in 1 Kings 10:18

> 1Kings 10:18 Moreover, the king made a great throne of ªivory and overlaid it with refined gold.

The Targum lists the following as accomplishments of Solomon: the Temple at Jerusalem, the royal summer palace, the chamber, the porch, the courthouse of hewn stones where the sages and judges sit in judgment and the ivory throne. Solomon also planted vineyards so that the rabbis and the Sanhedrin could drink together with the King.[15]

4. What country did the slaves come from? (v. 7)

The Targum states that the slaves were from the House of Ham, one of Noah's sons. Noah cursed Ham and said that the descendants of Shem would rule over the descendants of Ham.

---

[13] Nosson Scherman and Meir Zlotowitz, *The Book of Megillos: the Five Megillos: a New Translation with Overviews and Annotations Anthologized from the Classical Commentators* (Brooklyn, NY: Mesorah Publications, 1986).
[14] IBID.
[15] Martin McNamara et al., *The Aramaic Bible. the Targums: The Targum of Job, the Targum of Proverbs, the Targum of Qohelet*, 1991.

5. What does verse twelve mean?

According to the Targum, this verse says that once a decree has been offered by the King, and after punishment for a crime is implemented, praying for a change will cause nothing.

6. What is the meaning of verse fourteen?

The sage Ibn Ezra[i] said that when a wise man and a foolish man set out to travel to the same destination, the wise man will take the direct route. The foolish man travels in odd directions because he is not sure of the correct path. He is groping in the dark, not knowing where he is stumbling.[16]

7. What does verse fifteen mean?

The Targum states that Solomon asked himself if he was to suffer the same fate as King Saul did because he did not keep the LORD's commandments concerning Amalek. Saul was supposed to wait for Samuel to advise him and instead sought out a witch. The Kingdom of Israel was taken away from Saul and his descendants for this sin. Solomon said that the LORD could take away his kingdom if he sinned in the same manner as Saul. Solomon was a fool who was supporting his vanity because he believed that the LORD would not take the nation away from him no matter what he did.

8. What is Solomon saying in verse seventeen

The Targum states that Solomon did not hate life but rather hated an evil life. His distress was concerning evil people in his kingdom who were doing evil deeds.

---

[16] Nosson Scherman and Meir Zlotowitz, *The Book of Megillos: the Five Megillos: a New Translation with Overviews and Annotations Anthologized from the Classical Commentators* (Brooklyn, NY: Mesorah Publications, 1986).

9. What does verse eighteen mean?

Solomon is referring to all the work he did to secure the Kingdom of Israel. His work was destroyed by his son Rehoboam. Solomon is saying that all his hard work to enlarge the Kingdom of Israel and bring peace to the land was pointless because his son would cause the Kingdom's destruction. This topic continues into verse nineteen. Perhaps Solomon was contemplating having a different heir to the throne.

It is vanity to think that one's children will continue the success and policies of the parent. Solomon acknowledged that all his work was for nothing if his son tried to administer the kingdom oppositely.

10. What is verse twenty-two to twenty-six referring to?

King Solomon recounts the need to place Torah learning and study above all else. The things a person creates or secures during their lifetime will eventually turn to dust. One's study and understanding of the Torah will enable a person to go to the world to come and be ready to meet the LORD.

Culture Section

Discussion

People during the time of Solomon's reign were unaware that there was life in the world to come, the afterlife. King Solomon had every luxury a man of his time could ask. Even with all the materials, wives, children, and more, he was still bored with life. Solomon, like other people of his time, thought that when they died, they were cut off from the LORD. Therefore, only their property would live on so that people would remember them. Solomon's grand Temple to the LORD, nor any of his material items, survived for us to enjoy today. What did survive is Solomon's words of wisdom found in this book and other writings. Being a righteous person and contributing to society is a way that a person's legacy lives on.[17]

Darkness is considered a lack of wisdom. Since wisdom comes from the LORD, then darkness is the absence of the presence of the LORD in one's life.

Thoughts

In this chapter, King Solomon continues to lament about a life filled with vanity. It was vanity to build the elaborate Temple in Jerusalem to show the LORD how fancy a house he could create for the LORD. The wives and concubines kept Solomon away from studying the Word of the LORD. All the vanity that existed in his administration was because he forced his people to build marvelous buildings and gardens. How did any of this work help anyone to be ready to go to Heaven? None of it did. Ask yourself, what labor could you stop so that you can use the time to learn more about the LORD?

---

[17] Rocco A. Errico and George M. Lamsa, *Aramaic Light on Ezra through the Song of Solomon* (Smyma, GA: Noohra Foundation, 2010).

Chapter Three

Language

New American Standard 1995	Hebrew
[1] There is an appointed time for everything. And there is a time for every event under heaven-- [2] A time to give birth and a time to die; A time to plant and a time to uproot what is planted. [3] A time to kill and a time to heal; A time to tear down and a time to build up. [4] A time to weep and a time to laugh; A time to mourn and a time to dance. [5] A time to throw stones and a time to gather stones; A time to embrace and a time to shun embracing. [6] A time to search and a time to give up as lost; A time to keep and a time to throw away. [7] A time to tear apart and a time to sew together; A time to be silent and a time to speak. [8] A time to love and a time to hate; A time for war and a time for peace. [9] What profit is there to the worker from that in which he toils? [10] I have seen the task which God has given the sons of men with which to occupy themselves. [11] He has made everything appropriate in its time. He has also set eternity in their heart, yet so that man will not find out the work which God has done from the beginning even to the end. [12] I know that there is nothing better for them than to rejoice and to do good in one's lifetime;	לַכֹּל זְמָן וְעֵת לְכָל־חֵפֶץ תַּחַת הַשָּׁמָיִם׃ ס [2] [1] עֵת לָלֶדֶת וְעֵת לָמוּת עֵת לָטַעַת וְעֵת לַעֲקוֹר נָטוּעַ׃ עֵת לַהֲרוֹג וְעֵת לִרְפּוֹא עֵת לִפְרוֹץ וְעֵת לִבְנוֹת׃ [3] עֵת לִבְכּוֹת וְעֵת לִשְׂחוֹק עֵת סְפוֹד וְעֵת רְקוֹד׃ [4] עֵת לְהַשְׁלִיךְ אֲבָנִים וְעֵת כְּנוֹס אֲבָנִים עֵת לַחֲבוֹק וְעֵת לִרְחֹק מֵחַבֵּק׃ [5] עֵת לְבַקֵּשׁ וְעֵת לְאַבֵּד עֵת לִשְׁמוֹר וְעֵת לְהַשְׁלִיךְ׃ [6] עֵת לִקְרוֹעַ וְעֵת לִתְפּוֹר עֵת לַחֲשׁוֹת וְעֵת לְדַבֵּר׃ [7] עֵת לֶאֱהֹב וְעֵת לִשְׂנֹא עֵת מִלְחָמָה וְעֵת שָׁלוֹם׃ ס [8] מַה־יִּתְרוֹן הָעוֹשֶׂה בַּאֲשֶׁר הוּא עָמֵל׃ [9] רָאִיתִי אֶת־הָעִנְיָן אֲשֶׁר נָתַן אֱלֹהִים לִבְנֵי הָאָדָם לַעֲנוֹת בּוֹ׃ [10] אֶת־הַכֹּל עָשָׂה יָפֶה בְעִתּוֹ גַּם אֶת־הָעֹלָם נָתַן בְּלִבָּם מִבְּלִי אֲשֶׁר לֹא־יִמְצָא הָאָדָם אֶת־הַמַּעֲשֶׂה אֲשֶׁר־עָשָׂה הָאֱלֹהִים מֵרֹאשׁ וְעַד־סוֹף׃ [11] יָדַעְתִּי כִּי אֵין טוֹב בָּם כִּי אִם־לִשְׂמוֹחַ וְלַעֲשׂוֹת טוֹב בְּחַיָּיו׃ [12] וְגַם כָּל־הָאָדָם שֶׁיֹּאכַל וְשָׁתָה וְרָאָה טוֹב בְּכָל־עֲמָלוֹ מַתַּת אֱלֹהִים הִיא׃ [13] יָדַעְתִּי כִּי כָּל־אֲשֶׁר יַעֲשֶׂה הָאֱלֹהִים הוּא יִהְיֶה לְעוֹלָם עָלָיו אֵין לְהוֹסִיף וּמִמֶּנּוּ אֵין לִגְרֹעַ וְהָאֱלֹהִים עָשָׂה שֶׁיִּרְאוּ מִלְּפָנָיו׃ [14] מַה־שֶּׁהָיָה כְּבָר הוּא וַאֲשֶׁר לִהְיוֹת כְּבָר הָיָה וְהָאֱלֹהִים יְבַקֵּשׁ אֶת־נִרְדָּף׃ [15] וְעוֹד רָאִיתִי תַּחַת הַשָּׁמֶשׁ מְקוֹם הַמִּשְׁפָּט שָׁמָּה הָרֶשַׁע וּמְקוֹם הַצֶּדֶק שָׁמָּה הָרָשַׁע׃ [16]

[13] moreover, that every man who eats and drinks sees good in all his labor-- it is the gift of God.

[14] I know that everything God does will remain forever; there is nothing to add to it and there is nothing to take from it, for God has *so* worked that men should fear Him.

[15] That which is has been already and that which will be has already been, for God seeks what has passed by.

[16] Furthermore, I have seen under the sun *that* in the place of justice there is wickedness and in the place of righteousness there is wickedness.

[17] I said to myself, "God will judge both the righteous man and the wicked man," for a time for every matter and for every deed is there.

[18] I said to myself concerning the sons of men, "God has surely tested them in order for them to see that they are but beasts."

[19] For the fate of the sons of men and the fate of beasts is the same. As one dies so dies the other; indeed, they all have the same breath and there is no advantage for man over beast, for all is vanity.

[20] All go to the same place. All came from the dust and all return to the dust.

[21] Who knows that the breath of man ascends upward and the breath of the beast descends downward to the earth?

[22] I have seen that nothing is better than that man should be happy in his activities, for that is his lot. For who will bring him to see what will occur after him?

‏[17] אָמַרְתִּי אֲנִי בְּלִבִּי אֶת־הַצַּדִּיק וְאֶת־הָרָשָׁע יִשְׁפֹּט הָאֱלֹהִים כִּי־עֵת לְכָל־חֵפֶץ וְעַל כָּל־הַמַּעֲשֶׂה שָׁם:

‏[18] אָמַרְתִּי אֲנִי בְּלִבִּי עַל־דִּבְרַת בְּנֵי הָאָדָם לְבָרָם הָאֱלֹהִים וְלִרְאוֹת שְׁהֶם־בְּהֵמָה הֵמָּה לָהֶם:

‏[19] כִּי מִקְרֶה בְנֵי־הָאָדָם וּמִקְרֶה הַבְּהֵמָה וּמִקְרֶה אֶחָד לָהֶם כְּמוֹת זֶה כֵּן מוֹת זֶה וְרוּחַ אֶחָד לַכֹּל וּמוֹתַר הָאָדָם מִן־הַבְּהֵמָה אָיִן כִּי הַכֹּל הָבֶל:

‏[20] הַכֹּל הוֹלֵךְ אֶל־מָקוֹם אֶחָד הַכֹּל הָיָה מִן־הֶעָפָר וְהַכֹּל שָׁב אֶל־הֶעָפָר:

‏[21] מִי יוֹדֵעַ רוּחַ בְּנֵי הָאָדָם הָעֹלָה הִיא לְמָעְלָה וְרוּחַ הַבְּהֵמָה הַיֹּרֶדֶת הִיא לְמַטָּה לָאָרֶץ:

‏[22] וְרָאִיתִי כִּי אֵין טוֹב מֵאֲשֶׁר יִשְׂמַח הָאָדָם בְּמַעֲשָׂיו כִּי־הוּא חֶלְקוֹ כִּי מִי יְבִיאֶנּוּ לִרְאוֹת בְּמֶה שֶׁיִּהְיֶה אַחֲרָיו:

Process of Discovery

Linguistics Section

Linguistic Structure

[Declarations] [1] There is an appointed time for everything. And there is a time for every event under heaven-- [2] A time to give birth and a time to die; A time to plant and a time to uproot what is planted. [3] A time to kill and a time to heal; A time to tear down and a time to build up. [4] A time to weep and a time to laugh; A time to mourn and a time to dance. [5] A time to throw stones and a time to gather stones; A time to embrace and a time to shun embracing. [6] A time to search and a time to give up as lost; A time to keep and a time to throw away. [7] A time to tear apart and a time to sew together; A time to be silent and a time to speak. [8] A time to love and a time to hate; A time for war and a time for peace.

A [9] What profit is there to the worker from that in which he toils?

> **B** [10] I have seen the task which God has given the sons of men with which to occupy themselves. [11] He has made everything appropriate in its time. He has also set eternity in their heart, yet so that man will not find out the work which God has done from the beginning even to the end.

A' [12] I know that there is nothing better for them than to rejoice and to do good in one's lifetime; [13] moreover, that every man who eats and drinks sees good in all his labor-- it is the gift of God.

A [14] I know that everything God does will remain forever; there is nothing to add to it and there is nothing to take from it, for God has *so* worked that men should fear Him. [15] That which is has been already and that which will be has already been, for God seeks what has passed by. [16] Furthermore, I have seen under the sun *that* in the place of justice there is wickedness and in the place of righteousness there is wickedness.

> **B** [17] I said to myself, "God will judge both the righteous man and the wicked man," for a time for every matter and for every deed is there. [18] I said to myself concerning the sons of men, "God has surely tested them in order for them to see that they are but beasts."

B' [19] For the fate of the sons of men and the fate of beasts is the same. As one dies so dies the other; indeed, they all have the same breath and there is no advantage for man over beast, for all is vanity. [20] All go to the same place. All came from the dust and all return to the dust.

A' [21] Who knows that the breath of man ascends upward and the breath of the beast descends downward to the earth? [22] I have seen that nothing is better than that man should be happy in his activities, for that is his lot. For who will bring him to see what will occur after him?

Discussion

This chapter consists of a chiasm with two centers.

Questioning the Passage

1. What does "set eternity in their heart" in verse eleven mean?

   The Sage Rashi[ii] said that this verse meant that the LORD instilled worldly wisdom into the hearts of humans. However, the LORD did not teach all aspects of wisdom. Instead, the LORD dispensed small amounts to each person so that no one would grasp the workings of God fully, or foresee the future. This method was done to ensure that people would repent from their sins.[18]

---

[18] Nosson Scherman and Meir Zlotowitz, *The Book of Megillos: the Five Megillos: a New Translation with Overviews and Annotations Anthologized from the Classical Commentators* (Brooklyn, NY: Mesorah Publications, 1986).

2. What is good to do over one's lifetime? (v. 12)

The joy King Solomon was speaking of is the study of the Torah. Studying the Word of the LORD enables a person to live a fruitful and prosperous life.

3. What does it mean that there is wickedness in a place of justice? (v. 16)

The Targum states that King Solomon understood that there were judges in his kingdom who declared the innocent guilty and the guilty innocent. There was corruption in the court system of Israel. Verse seventeen says that Solomon understood that the final judgment is from the LORD who will offer true justice. The LORD will judge every person for what they have done. Justice will come to those who were judged unfairly and judgment will be rendered to those who abuse the court system.

4. Whom is verse nineteen referring to?

According to the Targum, people guilty of sins will suffer the same fate as an unclean animal does. The Bible does not offer what the future of unclean animals are. The inference in the Targum is that the guilty person who does not repent of their sins before death does not have the opportunity to offer repentance to the LORD in the end. In the same way that an unclean animal will never be able to become clean.

Culture Section

Discussion

Time is addressed first in the declarations. Time does not exist in the realm of Heaven. Time is marked on Earth by the movement of the planets, moon, and the stars. Genesis says that the LORD created the heavenly bodies to mark the days, months and years. Humans work and develop events to correspond to the time calendar. Time is the most precious thing humans have. King Solomon suggested that humans recognize the time and not waste a single moment of it on foolishness.

Additional Information from the Targum

The second declaration about a time to give birth and a time to die is elaborated in the Targum as "A time chosen to bear sons and a time chosen to kill rebellious and blaspheming sons, to kill them with stones by order of the judges." King Solomon might have been thinking about his half brother that his father King David had to kill. Absalom led a revolt against David, and when the revolution was silenced, David had Absalom executed. It had to be difficult for David to kill his son. Nevertheless, for the sake of his power on the throne of Israel David had no choice.

Verse three in the Targum reads, "A time chosen to kill in battle and a time chosen to cure the critically ill." The murder of a member of the tribe is unacceptable, as stated in the Ten Commandments. Solomon was speaking about the need to kill an enemy in battle.

Verse four in the Targum reads, "A time to weep over a dead person and time chose to rejoice with laughter." The Targum tightens when they need it is time to weep. Weeping was done over the death of a loved one or friend.

Verse five, second half, in the Targum reads, "A time chosen to embrace a wife and a time chosen to refrain from embracing a wife during the seven days of mourning."

The seven days of mourning is called *Shiva*. "Shiva begins immediately following the burial and lasts for seven days, ending after the morning service on the seventh day. Shiva is not observed on the Sabbath (Friday at sundown through Saturday at sundown) or holidays. While shiva is the seven days following burial – and many mourners do choose to observe shiva for the full seven days – it is common to find that some families may only **sit shiva** for one-to-three days, depending on many factors, including the family's level of observance or the deceased's instructions or wishes."[19] During the seven days of mourning, it is wrong for spouses to embrace (have sex). The deceased must be remembered during the shiva time. No activity should be done, which takes one away from this obligation.

Verse six in the Targum reads, "A time chosen to seek property and a time chosen to lose the property. A time was ch sen to keep merchandise and time chosen to throw merchandise into the sea at a time of a storm." Verse six refers to property. In the ancient world in Israel, there were times of peace and times of war. During times of peace, people could gather possessions. When an enemy decided to attack a family could lose everything they owned and their land. The times of attacks were unknown to the average person working on their farm. The latter part could be referring to when a storm hits a ship on the sea. Sometimes the merchandise on the ship has to be sacrificed for the boat to survive. The first chapter of the book of Jonah is a good example of this situation.

The first part of verse seven in the Targum reads, "A time to rend a garment over a dead person and time chosen to mend that which was rent." When Jewish people

---

[19] "How Is Shiva Observed," Shiva, Jewish Mourning, accessed January 16, 2020, https://www.shiva.com/learning-center/understanding/how-shiva-observed/.

mourn for a loved one, they will tear a piece of clothing. When the time of mourning passes, the garment can be repaired.

Thoughts

During Solomon's time, people did not understand the concept of immortality. The idea of living for the World to Come did not exist. Therefore judgment for one's action on Earth needed to be done by the court system. Unfortunately, Solomon knew that his court system was corrupt. He hints that the LORD will be the ultimate judge. That would mean that the LORD has His hand in the daily affairs of people. When a sinner does not repent, the LORD could send "bad luck" his way.

The key to this chapter is that humans mark time. There is a time for all of the activities of humans. Time was created by the LORD and scored in the sky by the heavenly luminaries. By the placement of the stars, the people knew when it was time to do things. This was important in ancient times because the people did not have a written calendar to mark time. Planting seeds at the wrong time of the year could cause a famine. By knowing the time of year via the stars, the farmers knew when to plant a seed and when to harvest.

All of human life is marked by time. Even today, we mark the passage of time with rituals, privileges, and at the end of life the removal of rights. Solomon knew that time was short and is telling us to live every minute because time is something you cannot buyback.

Chapter Four

Language

New American Standard 1995	Hebrew
[1] Then I looked again at all the acts of oppression which were being done under the sun. And behold *I saw* the tears of the oppressed and *that* they had no one to comfort *them*; and on the side of their oppressors was power, but they had no one to comfort *them*. [2] So I congratulated the dead who are already dead more than the living who are still living. [3] But better *off* than both of them is the one who has never existed, who has never seen the evil activity that is done under the sun. [4] I have seen that every labor and every skill which is done is *the result of* rivalry between a man and his neighbor. This too is vanity and striving after wind. [5] The fool folds his hands and consumes his own flesh. [6] One hand full of rest is better than two fists full of labor and striving after wind. [7] Then I looked again at vanity under the sun. [8] There was a certain man without a dependent, having neither a son nor a brother, yet there was no end to all his labor. Indeed, his eyes were not satisfied with riches *and he never asked*, "And for whom am I laboring and depriving myself	וְשַׁבְתִּי אֲנִי וָאֶרְאֶה אֶת־כָּל־הָעֲשֻׁקִים אֲשֶׁר נַעֲשִׂים תַּחַת הַשָּׁמֶשׁ וְהִנֵּה דִּמְעַת הָעֲשֻׁקִים וְאֵין לָהֶם מְנַחֵם וּמִיַּד עֹשְׁקֵיהֶם כֹּחַ וְאֵין לָהֶם מְנַחֵם: [2] וְשַׁבֵּחַ אֲנִי אֶת־הַמֵּתִים שֶׁכְּבָר מֵתוּ מִן־הַחַיִּים אֲשֶׁר הֵמָּה חַיִּים עֲדֶנָה: [3] וְטוֹב מִשְּׁנֵיהֶם אֵת אֲשֶׁר־עֲדֶן לֹא הָיָה אֲשֶׁר לֹא־רָאָה אֶת־הַמַּעֲשֶׂה הָרָע אֲשֶׁר נַעֲשָׂה תַּחַת הַשָּׁמֶשׁ: [4] וְרָאִיתִי אֲנִי אֶת־כָּל־עָמָל וְאֵת כָּל־כִּשְׁרוֹן הַמַּעֲשֶׂה כִּי הִיא קִנְאַת־אִישׁ מֵרֵעֵהוּ גַּם־זֶה הֶבֶל וּרְעוּת רוּחַ: [5] הַכְּסִיל חֹבֵק אֶת־יָדָיו וְאֹכֵל אֶת־בְּשָׂרוֹ: [6] טוֹב מְלֹא כַף נָחַת מִמְּלֹא חָפְנַיִם עָמָל וּרְעוּת רוּחַ: [7] וְשַׁבְתִּי אֲנִי וָאֶרְאֶה הֶבֶל תַּחַת הַשָּׁמֶשׁ: [8] יֵשׁ אֶחָד וְאֵין שֵׁנִי גַּם בֵּן וָאָח אֵין־לוֹ וְאֵין קֵץ לְכָל־עֲמָלוֹ גַּם־(עיניו) [עֵינוֹ] לֹא־תִשְׂבַּע עֹשֶׁר וּלְמִי אֲנִי עָמֵל וּמְחַסֵּר אֶת־נַפְשִׁי מִטּוֹבָה גַּם־זֶה הֶבֶל וְעִנְיַן רָע הוּא: [9] טוֹבִים הַשְּׁנַיִם מִן־הָאֶחָד אֲשֶׁר יֵשׁ־לָהֶם שָׂכָר טוֹב בַּעֲמָלָם: [10] כִּי אִם־יִפֹּלוּ הָאֶחָד יָקִים אֶת־חֲבֵרוֹ וְאִילוֹ הָאֶחָד שֶׁיִּפּוֹל וְאֵין שֵׁנִי לַהֲקִימוֹ: [11] גַּם אִם־יִשְׁכְּבוּ שְׁנַיִם וְחַם לָהֶם וּלְאֶחָד אֵיךְ יֵחָם: [12] וְאִם־יִתְקְפוֹ הָאֶחָד הַשְּׁנַיִם יַעַמְדוּ נֶגְדּוֹ וְהַחוּט הַמְשֻׁלָּשׁ לֹא בִמְהֵרָה יִנָּתֵק: [13] טוֹב יֶלֶד מִסְכֵּן וְחָכָם מִמֶּלֶךְ זָקֵן וּכְסִיל אֲשֶׁר לֹא־יָדַע לְהִזָּהֵר עוֹד:

of pleasure?" This too is vanity and it is a grievous task.

⁹ Two are better than one because they have a good return for their labor.

¹⁰ For if either of them falls, the one will lift up his companion. But woe to the one who falls when there is not another to lift him up.

¹¹ Furthermore, if two lie down together they keep warm, but how can one be warm *alone*?

¹² And if one can overpower him who is alone, two can resist him. A cord of three *strands* is not quickly torn apart.

¹³ A poor yet wise lad is better than an old and foolish king who no longer knows *how* to receive instruction.

¹⁴ For he has come out of prison to become king, even though he was born poor in his kingdom.

¹⁵ I have seen all the living under the sun throng to the side of the second lad who replaces him.

¹⁶ There is no end to all the people, to all who were before them, and even the ones who will come later will not be happy with him, for this too is vanity and striving after wind.

כִּֽי־מִבֵּית הָסוּרִים יָצָא לִמְלֹךְ כִּי גַם בְּמַלְכוּתוֹ נוֹלַד רָשׁ: ¹⁴

רָאִיתִי אֶת־כָּל־הַחַיִּים הַמְהַלְּכִים תַּחַת הַשָּׁמֶשׁ עִם הַיֶּלֶד הַשֵּׁנִי אֲשֶׁר יַעֲמֹד תַּחְתָּיו: ¹⁵

אֵֽין־קֵץ לְכָל־הָעָם לְכֹל אֲשֶׁר־הָיָה לִפְנֵיהֶם גַּם הָאַחֲרוֹנִים לֹא יִשְׂמְחוּ־בוֹ כִּי־גַם־זֶה הֶבֶל וְרַעְיוֹן רוּחַ: ¹⁶

שְׁמֹר (רגליך) [רַגְלְךָ] כַּאֲשֶׁר תֵּלֵךְ אֶל־בֵּית הָאֱלֹהִים וְקָרוֹב לִשְׁמֹעַ מִתֵּת הַכְּסִילִים זָבַח כִּֽי־אֵינָם יוֹדְעִים לַעֲשׂוֹת רָע: ¹⁷

Process of Discovery

Linguistics Section

Linguistic Structure

A [1] Then I looked again at all the acts of oppression which were being done under the sun. And behold *I saw* the tears of the oppressed and *that* they had no one to comfort *them*; and on the side of their oppressors was power, but they had no one to comfort *them*.

    B [2] So I congratulated the dead who are already dead more than the living who are still living.

    B' [3] But better *off* than both of them is the one who has never existed, who has never seen the evil activity that is done under the sun.

A' [4] I have seen that every labor and every skill which is done is *the result of* rivalry between a man and his neighbor. This too is vanity and striving after wind. [5] The fool folds his hands and consumes his own flesh. [6] One hand full of rest is better than two fists full of labor and striving after wind.

A: Hands. B: Happiness.[20]

[Statement] [7] Then I looked again at vanity under the sun. [8] There was a certain man without a dependent, having neither a son nor a brother, yet there was no end to all his labor. Indeed, his eyes were not satisfied with riches *and he never asked*, "And for whom am I laboring and depriving myself of pleasure?" This too is vanity and it is a grievous task.

[Sayings] [9] Two are better than one because they have a good return for their labor. [10] For if either of them falls, the one will lift up his companion. But woe to the one who falls when there is not another to lift him up.

---

[20] Hajime Murai, "Literary Structure (Chiasm, Chiasmus) of Ecclesiastes," Literary structure (chiasm, chiasmus) of each pericopes of Ecclesiastes, accessed January 18, 2020, http://www.bible.literarystructure.info/bible/21_Ecclesiastes_pericope_e.html#7.

[Sayings] [11] Furthermore, if two lie down together they keep warm, but how can one be warm *alone*?

[Sayings] [12] And if one can overpower him who is alone, two can resist him. A cord of three *strands* is not quickly torn apart.

[Sayings] [13] A poor yet wise lad is better than an old and foolish king who no longer knows *how* to receive instruction. [14] For he has come out of prison to become king, even though he was born poor in his kingdom.

[Sayings] [15] I have seen all the living under the sun throng to the side of the second lad who replaces him. [16] There is no end to all the people, to all who were before them, and even the ones who will come later will not be happy with him, for this too is vanity and striving after wind.

Discussion

This chapter commences with a short chiasm. It then offers a question which is answered by the five sayings that follow it.

Questioning the Passage

1. Why did the author congratulate the dead in verse two?

   The Sage Rav Yosef Kara[iii] said that this verse means that the dead who were exposed to social injustice is more fortunate than the living because social injustice cannot affect them.[21]

---

[21] Nosson Scherman and Meir Zlotowitz, *The Book of Megillos: the Five Megillos: a New Translation with Overviews and Annotations Anthologized from the Classical Commentators* (Brooklyn, NY: Mesorah Publications, 1986).

2. Why are those who never existed better off, as indicated in verse three?

Rav Yosef Kara said the most fortunate souls are those who have not been born because they will never suffer social injustice.[22]

3. What does it mean that a man worked without a dependent, therefore there is no end to all his labor? (v. 8)

The Targum says this verse is referring to a person who worked their entire life and has no heir to give an inheritance. Therefore, there is no end to all of his labors. This person continues to work and accumulate wealth. If the person has no heir, he/she will probably give the wealth to charity. Announcing that this is going to be done is vanity, according to the author.

4. What does the statement "two are better than one" in verse nine mean?

This statement is referring to the number of righteous persons in a generation. The Zohar says that there is always one righteous person in every age. Solomon tells us that it is much better to have two righteous men sent by the LORD. The righteous labor to bring righteousness to as many people as possible. Two or more righteous persons would bring double plus the number of blessings from the LORD. In verse ten, the Targum says if there are two righteous persons in a generation if one takes ill, the other can pray for healing and recovery. If there is only one righteous person in a generation, the fallen righteous person would have to heal themselves which is more complicated. There is added strength from the prayer of others when combined with one's prayer (this is found in the Zohar).

---

[22] IBID.

5. What is verse eleven referring to?

The Targum states that the two who lie down together are a husband and his wife. They would engage in marital activities to keep warm. The rest of the verse is saying that a man or woman alone cannot participate in sex in the same manner.

6. What is verse twelve saying?

The Targum states that if a robust and wicked person arises in a generation that the LORD will send two righteous persons to annul the suffering that the evil person commits. In some ages, there will be three righteous persons who will combat the wicked person. They are like a three cord chain that cannot be easily broken.

7. Who is the poor wise lad in verse thirteen?

The Targum says that the wise lad was Abraham. He had the spirit of wisdom in him from the LORD and that the LORD became known to him at the age of three. Abraham did not want to worship idols. The wicked Nimrod, who was the King, old and foolish, threw Abraham into a furnace because Abraham did not believe in the idols of the King. Abraham survived the furnace, but that did not convince Nimrod to stop worshiping idols. The story continues in verse fourteen. Abraham came out of a family of idol worshipers, prison, and the LORD sent him to Canaan which prospered as land when Abraham lived there. The kingdom of Nimrod became poor after Abraham left Ur.

8. What does verse fifteen to seventeen mean?

The Targum states that Solomon was referring to the second in command of his kingdom who was Rehoboam. When Rehoboam became the King, the people of the north revolted against him. The ten tribes to the north were happier, allowing wicked Jeroboam to rule over them then Rehoboam. This view was a prophecy that the LORD gave Solomon. The ten tribes of the north chose to do evil instead of righteousness when they broke away. Solomon was also referring to the Davidic covenant. A son of the line of David would be the only King over Israel. After Solomon's death, Israel had two kings and that caused a problem because of the Davidic covenant.

Additional Information from the Targum

The Targum says that verse one is referring to the righteous of the world who were being oppressed by the hands of oppressors, and there was no way on Earth to stop it.

Verse four talks about the jealousy that one person has for another. It is envy that brings oppression. One who is envious or jealous of his neighbor will perform evil against his fellow person.

The Targum says that verse five is saying that a fool folds his hands in the summer when it is time to work the fields so that there will be a good harvest. In the winter, the clown eats whatever food he has but it will not be enough to quench hunger. The fool will then cast the clothing off his/her flesh.

Verse six says that it is better to have a handful of food with the pleasure of the soul without stealing the food because if the food is stolen, there will be a Final Judgment.

Thoughts

If anthropologists are correct, human civilizations started on the banks of the Tigris and Euphrates rivers. Small city-states emerged. Each city-state had different resources and knowledge of how to use specific resources. At times they shared but most of the time, they attacked each other to gain goods or the secrets of the usage of resources. How simple it would have been if they could have put their envy and jealousy aside and worked out trade deals. There were some trade deals but there was always some resource that a city-state would not share. Solomon said that it is the vanity that allows envy to take over. Eventually, city-states were brought together to form nations. Several groups of peoples/nations formed in the Middle East. These groups of people have been fighting and killing each other for many millennia. It was the British at the Treaty of Versailles, which ended World War I, which created the countries of the Middle East. The signers of the treaty did not understand the history of the people in the Middle East. They set up the troubles that are occurring today in the Middle East. In the Middle East, the primary resource is oil. Who has it and how much they have is what countries in that region are fighting over. Too bad they will not listen to the words of Solomon.

Chapter Five

Language

New Standard America 1995	Hebrew
[1] Guard your steps as you go to the house of God and draw near to listen rather than to offer the sacrifice of fools; for they do not know they are doing evil.	¹אַל־תְּבַהֵל עַל־פִּיךָ וְלִבְּךָ אַל־יְמַהֵר לְהוֹצִיא דָבָר לִפְנֵי הָאֱלֹהִים כִּי הָאֱלֹהִים בַּשָּׁמַיִם וְאַתָּה עַל־הָאָרֶץ עַל־כֵּן יִהְיוּ דְבָרֶיךָ מְעַטִּים:
[2] Do not be hasty in word or impulsive in thought to bring up a matter in the presence of God. For God is in heaven and you are on the earth; therefore let your words be few.	²כִּי בָּא הַחֲלוֹם בְּרֹב עִנְיָן וְקוֹל כְּסִיל בְּרֹב דְּבָרִים:
[3] For the dream comes through much effort and the voice of a fool through many words.	³כַּאֲשֶׁר תִּדֹּר נֶדֶר לֵאלֹהִים אַל־תְּאַחֵר לְשַׁלְּמוֹ כִּי אֵין חֵפֶץ בַּכְּסִילִים אֵת אֲשֶׁר־תִּדֹּר שַׁלֵּם:
[4] When you make a vow to God, do not be late in paying it; for *He takes* no delight in fools. Pay what you vow!	⁴טוֹב אֲשֶׁר לֹא־תִדֹּר מִשֶּׁתִּדּוֹר וְלֹא תְשַׁלֵּם:
[5] It is better that you should not vow than that you should vow and not pay.	⁵אַל־תִּתֵּן אֶת־פִּיךָ לַחֲטִיא אֶת־בְּשָׂרֶךָ וְאַל־תֹּאמַר לִפְנֵי הַמַּלְאָךְ כִּי שְׁגָגָה הִיא לָמָּה יִקְצֹף הָאֱלֹהִים עַל־קוֹלֶךָ וְחִבֵּל אֶת־מַעֲשֵׂה יָדֶיךָ:
[6] Do not let your speech cause you to sin and do not say in the presence of the messenger *of God* that it was a mistake. Why should God be angry on account of your voice and destroy the work of your hands?	⁶כִּי בְרֹב חֲלֹמוֹת וַהֲבָלִים וּדְבָרִים הַרְבֵּה כִּי אֶת־הָאֱלֹהִים יְרָא:
[7] For in many dreams and in many words there is emptiness. Rather, fear God.	⁷אִם־עֹשֶׁק רָשׁ וְגֵזֶל מִשְׁפָּט וָצֶדֶק תִּרְאֶה בַמְּדִינָה אַל־תִּתְמַהּ עַל־הַחֵפֶץ כִּי גָבֹהַּ מֵעַל גָּבֹהַּ שֹׁמֵר וּגְבֹהִים עֲלֵיהֶם:
[8] If you see oppression of the poor and denial of justice and righteousness in the province, do not be shocked at the sight; for one official watches over another official, and there are higher officials over them.	⁸וְיִתְרוֹן אֶרֶץ בַּכֹּל (היא) [הוּא] מֶלֶךְ לְשָׂדֶה נֶעֱבָד:
	⁹אֹהֵב כֶּסֶף לֹא־יִשְׂבַּע כֶּסֶף וּמִי־אֹהֵב בֶּהָמוֹן לֹא תְבוּאָה גַּם־זֶה הָבֶל:
	¹⁰בִּרְבוֹת הַטּוֹבָה רַבּוּ אוֹכְלֶיהָ וּמַה־כִּשְׁרוֹן לִבְעָלֶיהָ כִּי אִם־(ראית) [רְאוּת] עֵינָיו:

9 After all, a king who cultivates the field is an advantage to the land.

10 He who loves money will not be satisfied with money, nor he who loves abundance *with its* income. This too is vanity.

11 When good things increase, those who consume them increase. So what is the advantage to their owners except to look on?

12 The sleep of the working man is pleasant, whether he eats little or much; but the full stomach of the rich man does not allow him to sleep.

13 There is a grievous evil *which* I have seen under the sun: riches being hoarded by their owner to his hurt.

14 When those riches were lost through a bad investment and he had fathered a son, then there was nothing to support him.

15 As he had come naked from his mother's womb, so will he return as he came. He will take nothing from the fruit of his labor that he can carry in his hand.

16 This also is a grievous evil-- exactly as a man is born, thus will he die. So what is the advantage to him who toils for the wind?

17 Throughout his life *he* also eats in darkness with great vexation, sickness and anger.

18 Here is what I have seen to be good and fitting: to eat, to drink and enjoy oneself in all one's labor in which he toils under the sun *during* the few years of his life which God has given him; for this is his reward.

19 Furthermore, as for every man to whom God has given riches and wealth, He has also empowered him to eat from

11 מְתוּקָה שְׁנַת הָעֹבֵד אִם־מְעַט וְאִם־הַרְבֵּה יֹאכֵל וְהַשָּׂבָע לֶעָשִׁיר אֵינֶנּוּ מַנִּיחַ לוֹ לִישׁוֹן:

12 יֵשׁ רָעָה חוֹלָה רָאִיתִי תַּחַת הַשָּׁמֶשׁ עֹשֶׁר שָׁמוּר לִבְעָלָיו לְרָעָתוֹ:

13 וְאָבַד הָעֹשֶׁר הַהוּא בְּעִנְיַן רָע וְהוֹלִיד בֵּן וְאֵין בְּיָדוֹ מְאוּמָה:

14 כַּאֲשֶׁר יָצָא מִבֶּטֶן אִמּוֹ עָרוֹם יָשׁוּב לָלֶכֶת כְּשֶׁבָּא וּמְאוּמָה לֹא־יִשָּׂא בַעֲמָלוֹ שֶׁיֹּלֵךְ בְּיָדוֹ:

15 וְגַם־זֹה רָעָה חוֹלָה כָּל־עֻמַּת שֶׁבָּא כֵּן יֵלֵךְ וּמַה־יִּתְרוֹן לוֹ שֶׁיַּעֲמֹל לָרוּחַ:

16 גַּם כָּל־יָמָיו בַּחֹשֶׁךְ יֹאכֵל וְכָעַס הַרְבֵּה וְחָלְיוֹ וָקָצֶף:

17 הִנֵּה אֲשֶׁר־רָאִיתִי אָנִי טוֹב אֲשֶׁר־יָפֶה לֶאֱכוֹל־וְלִשְׁתּוֹת וְלִרְאוֹת טוֹבָה בְּכָל־עֲמָלוֹ שֶׁיַּעֲמֹל תַּחַת־הַשָּׁמֶשׁ מִסְפַּר יְמֵי־(חַיָו) [חַיָּיו] אֲשֶׁר־נָתַן־לוֹ הָאֱלֹהִים כִּי־הוּא חֶלְקוֹ:

18 גַּם כָּל־הָאָדָם אֲשֶׁר נָתַן־לוֹ הָאֱלֹהִים עֹשֶׁר וּנְכָסִים וְהִשְׁלִיטוֹ לֶאֱכֹל מִמֶּנּוּ וְלָשֵׂאת אֶת־חֶלְקוֹ וְלִשְׂמֹחַ בַּעֲמָלוֹ זֹה מַתַּת אֱלֹהִים הִיא:

19 כִּי לֹא הַרְבֵּה יִזְכֹּר אֶת־יְמֵי חַיָּיו כִּי הָאֱלֹהִים מַעֲנֶה בְּשִׂמְחַת לִבּוֹ:

them and to receive his reward and rejoice in his labor; this is the gift of God. [20] For he will not often consider the years of his life, because God keeps him occupied with the gladness of his heart.

Process of Discovery

Linguistics Section

Linguistic Structure

[Advise] [1] Guard your steps as you go to the house of God and draw near to listen rather than to offer the sacrifice of fools; for they do not know they are doing evil. [2] Do not be hasty in word or impulsive in thought to bring up a matter in the presence of God. For God is in heaven and you are on the earth; therefore let your words be few. [3] For the dream comes through much effort and the voice of a fool through many words.

[Advise] [4] When you make a vow to God, do not be late in paying it; for *He takes* no delight in fools. Pay what you vow! [5] It is better that you should not vow than that you should vow and not pay. [6] Do not let your speech cause you to sin and do not say in the presence of the messenger *of God* that it was a mistake. Why should God be angry on account of your voice and destroy the work of your hands? [7] For in many dreams and in many words there is emptiness. Rather, fear God.

[Commandment] [8] If you see oppression of the poor and denial of justice and righteousness in the province, do not be shocked at the sight; for one official watches over another official, and there are higher officials over them. [9] After all, a king who cultivates the field is an advantage to the land.

[Advise] [10] He who loves money will not be satisfied with money, nor he who loves abundance *with its* income. This too is vanity.

[Advise] [11] When good things increase, those who consume them increase. So what is the advantage to their owners except to look on?

[Advise] [12] The sleep of the working man is pleasant, whether he eats little or much; but the full stomach of the rich man does not allow him to sleep.

[Observations] [13] There is a grievous evil *which* I have seen under the sun: riches being hoarded by their owner to his hurt. [14] When those riches were lost through a bad investment and he had fathered a son, then there was nothing to support him. [15] As he had come naked from his mother's womb, so will he return as he came. He will take nothing from the fruit of his labor that he can carry in his hand.[16] This also is a grievous evil-- exactly as a man is born, thus will he die. So what is the advantage to him who toils for the wind?[17] Throughout his life *he* also eats in darkness with great vexation, sickness and anger.

[Observations] [18] Here is what I have seen to be good and fitting: to eat, to drink and enjoy oneself in all one's labor in which he toils under the sun *during* the few years of his life which God has given him; for this is his reward.

[Observations] [19] Furthermore, as for every man to whom God has given riches and wealth, He has also empowered him to eat from them and to receive his reward and rejoice in his labor; this is the gift of God.[20] For he will not often consider the years of his life, because God keeps him occupied with the gladness of his heart.

Discussion

In the Hebrew version of Kohelet verse, 5:1 is 4:17. This chapter is filled with advice and observations of King Solomon.

Questioning the Passage

1. What does it mean to guard one's steps when going into the house of the LORD? (v. 1-3)

   This piece of advice applies to all parts of life. It means that humans must remember that it was the LORD who created the world and rules all aspects of it. Humans will never understand why the LORD set up things the way they were done.[23] The Targum adds that a person must not be rash with

---

[23] Nosson Scherman and Meir Zlotowitz, *The Book of Megillos: the Five Megillos: a New Translation with Overviews and Annotations Anthologized from the Classical Commentators* (Brooklyn, NY: Mesorah Publications, 1986).

utterances because a mistake may occur. It also says that one should not be in a hurry to say a prayer to the LORD, implying one must think before praying to the LORD.

2. What does verse six mean?

The reader is reminded that when one stands before the LORD on judgment day that the words uttered during one's lifetime cannot be taken back. Think before speaking, especially if it is against the LORD.

3. What does verse fourteen mean?

The Targum states that when a father gains his wealth through sin, i.e., cheating people so that he accumulates wealth, that justice may come after the father is dead, and it will be the son that has to give all of the wealth back to its actual owners. Thus, the son would be left penniless.

4. What does it mean to eat in darkness? (v. 17)

The Targum states that this means that this person was alone. Being alone creates a life of sorrow and despair. It is better, to be honest, genuine, and have family and friends; then, it is to be dishonest and have a great deal of wealth.

Phrase Study

1. נֶדֶר.

"Vow, votive offering. RSV superior to ASV at Lev 7:16; 22:18; etc., where the noun denotes the thing offered. This noun represents either the result of נָדַר, i.e. a vow, or the thing offered to fulfill a vow. For synonyms see

נֶדֶב. Cognates for the noun occur in Ugaritic and Phoenician, as for the verb (see above). The noun occurs fifty-nine times.

נֶדֶר occurs in the lists of sacrifices (e.g. Deut 12:6, 11) as a species of peace offering (Lev 7:16). A closer description occurs in Num 30:3 [H 4] where to נָדַר a נֶדֶר is to swear to God with an oath (הִשָּׁבַע שְׁבֻעָה; cf. Ps 132:2) and to bind one's self with what proceeds from one's mouth. A נֶדֶר is something promised to God verbally (Num 30:4 [H 5]). If one so promises he is obliged to fulfill/do his promise (Deut 23:22). In most cases, the context shows that the vow implies a promised gift for sacrifice, not merely a course of action as is implied in the English word "vow." The biblical "vow" is always to deity, never a promise between man and man. Rash vows are to be avoided (Prov 20:25; cf. Jud 11:30) as foolish (Eccl 5:4 [H 3]f.) in the fullest sense of that word. One is not bound, however, to make a vow (contract) with God, for not to do so is no sin (Deut 23:23 [H 24]). A נֶדֶר is a species of thank offering (made even by Gentiles, Nah 1:15 [H 2]) vowed (Ps 116:14, 18) in return for God's favor (Num 21:1–3) or as an expression of godly zeal and devotion and in praise for answered prayer (Ps 22:25 [H 26]). Happiness results when a vow is properly fulfilled (Job 22:27).

Almost anything that is not God's already (Lev 27:26; note the development in the concept of tithing, Gen 31:13), or an abomination to him (Deut 23:18 [H 19] — such as the wages of a male or female harlot; cf. Prov 7:14) — can be vowed. A person can even vow himself to service, or be vowed to service, and can be redeemed (or redeem himself) thus giving to God a value equal in worth to his actual service, but being free to pursue his own life (27:2ff.). Clean beasts which fulfilled a vow were presented as votive offerings [Vol. 2, p. 558] unless they did not fulfill the requirements otherwise specified in the law (27:9ff.; cf. 22:18ff.; נָדַב) in which case the offerer can also present a second acceptable offering. Both animals, however, are holy (27:9ff.). One is sacrificed, the other becomes the possession of the priesthood. Unclean beasts may be redeemed (27:11ff.). The regulations governing vowing a house or houses, and land also appear in Lev 27. During the wilderness wanderings (KD, Num 15:3) the amount of fine flour and drink offering to accompany the various kinds of animals potentially constituting votive offerings was stipulated.

The נֶדֶר could be a burnt offering (Lev 22:18) or a peace-offering, in which case it was to be eaten on either the first or second day (7:16). For more details see נָדַב and שְׁלָמִים.

Both men and women could make vows. This is tempered by an institutionalization of woman's submission to man (Num 30:4 [H 5]). Yet it is important to note that women could own property and be religiously responsible for themselves (30:9 [H 10]). The submission (Gen 2:21f.) sanctioned the family institution by emphasizing the importance of that union and relationship. After entry into Palestine the neder together with other stipulated sacrifices were to be consummated only at the designated central sanctuary (Deut 12:6, 11).

To make vows was not a religious duty (23:21–23 [H 22–24]). Such vows were acceptable to God (Ps 50:8). He makes it clear, however, that he is not being fed or tended (50:9–13) as paganism thought (cf. A. Leo Oppenheim, *Ancient Mesopotamia,* University of Chicago, 1964, p. 183ff.). Vows were supererogatory acts of devotion and love contracted either preceeding (50:14) or following divine blessing (116:17–18). They were accompanied by joy (Nah 1:5 [H 2:1] and/or singing (Ps 61:8 [H 9]), and were acceptable only if iniquity was not cherished in the offerer's heart (Ps 66:18; cf. Prov 7:14).

There are at least two noteworthy special vows: the Nazirite (Num 6:13ff; נֵזֶר, q.v.) and the חֵרֶם (21:2; חרם, q.v.). Absalom begged leave of David's court to fulfill a vow (2 Sam 15:7–8). The depth of his deceit is shown by both his having lied and having lied respecting divine ordinances. Elkanah on the other hand, both conscientiously fulfilled his own vows (1 Sam 1:21) and concurred with Hannah's (1:11, 22–23; Cf. Num 30). Jephthah's rash promise of a human sacrifice is inexcusable, however low the level of his knowledge of divine law. Thankfully, it was tempered when he dedicated his only daughter to lifelong service in the tabernacle, as seems at least possible (Jud 11:30, 39; cf. KD).

The נֵדֶר uniquely and concretely represents the love which conforms to divine pleasure showing that even in the Mosaic era love (Deut 6:4), and not pure legalism, best described true godliness. The Messiah is also bound by vow to offer himself a sacrifice for sin (Ps 22:25 [H 26]; cf. Lev. 27:2ff.)— the only human sacrifice truly "acceptable" to God. All men are to come to God with their vows (Ps 65:1 [H 2]; cf. Isa 19:21), and what can they bring as a votive offering other than God's own lamb (Jn 1:29)?"[24]

---

[24] TWOT electronic version from Accordance Bible Software V. 13

2. זֶבַח *(zābaḥ)* ***sacrifice, slaughter.***

This word is found in verse one.[25]

What if one thought about a vow as being equal to a sacrifice? When a promise is made to the LORD to do something, it usually involves some sacrifice. The sacrifice of fools is when a sacrifice was made at the altar of the LORD and the person turns around and commits the same sin again. Making a vow which involves the LORD or is to the LORD and then breaking it is the same as bringing a sacrifice to the altar because it is required, but the giver intends to sin again. Vow breaking is a sin and the connection is the word נֶדֶר meaning both.

Culture Section

Discussion

It was considered a sin to make a vow and not fulfill it in the Middle East. It was better not to make a vow that could not be fulfilled. Many times vows were made in the name of the LORD. Solomon said that it best not to make vows to the LORD. Vows are not a requirement of worshiping the LORD. Therefore, do not make vows.[26]

---

[25] IBID.

[26] Rocco A. Errico and George M. Lamsa, *Aramaic Light on Ezra through the Song of Solomon* (Smyma, GA: Noohra Foundation, 2010).

Additional Notes from the Targum

The Targum adds for verse eight that there is evil that will be done in this world. This evil is not the will of the LORD, nor is it something the LORD will tolerate. Instead, the LORD appointed powerful men and women to rule the wicked and to ensure that justice occurs. Sometimes a person has to get involved in ensuring that justice occurs.

The Targum states in verse nine that it is best when a king assists in the cultivation of his fields. If he does not get involved in the planting process, then there would not be any harvest. It is not beneath a king to get his hands dirty in a field. The workers of the field will feel respected if the king joins them while working in the fields.

Thoughts

It is interesting that sacrifice at the Temple, and a vow is connected linguistically. There had to be a belief that the two were connected spiritually for Hebrew to adopt the concurrent meanings. It is sinful to offer a vow to the LORD and then to break it. It is equivalent to bringing a sacrifice to the LORD and then repeating the sin. Everything that one does for the LORD today is a sacrifice. If one is tithing, then the sacrifice is that the individual could use the money for self-pleasure. Attending worship fellowships is a sacrifice of time. There is plenty to do in this world on the day of Shabbat. One who believes in the LORD will sacrifice doing tasks on the Shabbat. Do not make vows to the LORD that you will not fulfill. When the movie "The Passion of the Christ" was released there were many people who said they would change their lives and work for the Messiah Yeshua. Were are those people now? Looking at the current attendance problems in the United States church, it is clear that these people who made vows to the LORD have broken those vows. Many people gave money to the church at that time. However, where are they now? They decided that it was essential to have their earthly pleasures than to give to the work of the LORD.

Chapter Six

Language

New American Standard 1995	Hebrew

New American Standard 1995

1 There is an evil which I have seen under the sun and it is prevalent among men--

2 a man to whom God has given riches and wealth and honor so that his soul lacks nothing of all that he desires; yet God has not empowered him to eat from them, for a foreigner enjoys them. This is vanity and a severe affliction.

3 If a man fathers a hundred *children* and lives many years, however many they be, but his soul is not satisfied with good things and he does not even have a *proper* burial, *then* I say, "Better the miscarriage than he,

4 for it comes in futility and goes into obscurity; and its name is covered in obscurity.

5 "It never sees the sun and it never knows *anything*; it is better off than he.

6 "Even if the *other* man lives a thousand years twice and does not enjoy good things-- do not all go to one place?"

7 All a man's labor is for his mouth and yet the appetite is not satisfied.

8 For what advantage does the wise man have over the fool? What *advantage* does the poor man have, knowing *how* to walk before the living?

9 What the eyes see is better than what the soul desires. This too is futility and a striving after wind.

10 Whatever exists has already been named, and it is known what man is; for he cannot dispute with him who is stronger than he is.

Hebrew

¹ יֵשׁ רָעָה אֲשֶׁר רָאִיתִי תַּחַת הַשָּׁמֶשׁ וְרַבָּה הִיא עַל־הָאָדָם: ²אִישׁ אֲשֶׁר יִתֶּן־לוֹ הָאֱלֹהִים עֹשֶׁר וּנְכָסִים וְכָבוֹד וְאֵינֶנּוּ חָסֵר לְנַפְשׁוֹ מִכֹּל אֲשֶׁר־יִתְאַוֶּה וְלֹא־יַשְׁלִיטֶנּוּ הָאֱלֹהִים לֶאֱכֹל מִמֶּנּוּ כִּי אִישׁ נָכְרִי יֹאכְלֶנּוּ זֶה הֶבֶל וָחֳלִי רָע הוּא:

³ אִם־יוֹלִיד אִישׁ מֵאָה וְשָׁנִים רַבּוֹת יִחְיֶה וְרַבּ שֶׁיִּהְיוּ יְמֵי־שָׁנָיו וְנַפְשׁוֹ לֹא־תִשְׂבַּע מִן־הַטּוֹבָה וְגַם־קְבוּרָה לֹא־הָיְתָה לּוֹ אָמַרְתִּי טוֹב מִמֶּנּוּ הַנָּפֶל:

⁴ כִּי־בַהֶבֶל בָּא וּבַחֹשֶׁךְ יֵלֵךְ וּבַחֹשֶׁךְ שְׁמוֹ יְכֻסֶּה:

⁵ גַּם־שֶׁמֶשׁ לֹא־רָאָה וְלֹא יָדָע נַחַת לָזֶה מִזֶּה:

⁶ וְאִלּוּ חָיָה אֶלֶף שָׁנִים פַּעֲמַיִם וְטוֹבָה לֹא רָאָה הֲלֹא אֶל־מָקוֹם אֶחָד הַכֹּל הוֹלֵךְ:

⁷ כָּל־עֲמַל הָאָדָם לְפִיהוּ וְגַם־הַנֶּפֶשׁ לֹא תִמָּלֵא:

⁸ כִּי מַה־יּוֹתֵר לֶחָכָם מִן־הַכְּסִיל מַה־לֶּעָנִי יוֹדֵעַ לַהֲלֹךְ נֶגֶד הַחַיִּים:

⁹ טוֹב מַרְאֵה עֵינַיִם מֵהֲלָךְ־נָפֶשׁ גַּם־זֶה הֶבֶל וּרְעוּת רוּחַ:

¹⁰ מַה־שֶּׁהָיָה כְּבָר נִקְרָא שְׁמוֹ וְנוֹדָע אֲשֶׁר־הוּא אָדָם וְלֹא־יוּכַל לָדִין עִם (שֶׁהַתְּקִיף) [שֶׁתַּקִּיף] מִמֶּנּוּ:

¹¹ כִּי יֵשׁ־דְּבָרִים הַרְבֵּה מַרְבִּים הָבֶל מַה־יֹּתֵר לָאָדָם:

¹² כִּי מִי־יוֹדֵעַ מַה־טּוֹב לָאָדָם בַּחַיִּים מִסְפַּר יְמֵי־חַיֵּי הֶבְלוֹ וְיַעֲשֵׂם כַּצֵּל אֲשֶׁר מִי־יַגִּיד לָאָדָם מַה־יִּהְיֶה אַחֲרָיו תַּחַת הַשָּׁמֶשׁ:

[11] For there are many words which increase futility. What *then* is the advantage to a man?

[12] For who knows what is good for a man during *his* lifetime, *during* the few years of his futile life? He will spend them like a shadow. For who can tell a man what will be after him under the sun?

Process of Discovery

Linguistics Section

Linguistic Structure

A [1] There is an evil which I have seen under the sun and it is prevalent among men-- [2] a man to whom God has given riches and wealth and honor so that his soul lacks nothing of all that he desires; yet God has not empowered him to eat from them, for a foreigner enjoys them. This is vanity and a severe affliction.

> **B** [3] If a man fathers a hundred *children* and lives many years, however many they be, but his soul is not satisfied with good things and he does not even have a *proper* burial, *then* I say, "Better the miscarriage than he, [4] for it comes in futility and goes into obscurity; and its name is covered in obscurity.

> **B'** [5] "It never sees the sun and it never knows *anything*; it is better off than he. [6] "Even if the *other* man lives a thousand years twice and does not enjoy good things-- do not all go to one place?"

> **B"** [7] All a man's labor is for his mouth and yet the appetite is not satisfied. [8] For what advantage does the wise man have over the fool? What *advantage* does the poor man have, knowing *how* to walk before the living?

> **B'''** [9] What the eyes see is better than what the soul desires. This too is futility and a striving after wind. [10] Whatever exists has already been named, and it is known what man is; for he cannot dispute with him who is stronger than he is. [11] For there are many words which increase futility. What *then* is the advantage to a man?

A' [12] For who knows what is good for a man during *his* lifetime, *during* the few years of his futile life? He will spend them like a shadow. For who can tell a man what will be after him under the sun?

Discussion

This chapter is bracketed by verses 1-2 and 12. The question of being under the sun creates the chiasm. There are four sayings between the brackets.

Questioning the Passage

1. How can a person have wealth, but the LORD prevents the person from using it? (v. 1 & 2)

   The Targum offers an answer to this question. A person who has been gifted wealth by the LORD but sins will find that the wealth cannot be used. The Targum continues that such a person will die childless. In the Targum, the masculine form is used. Therefore, the Targum continues that the man's wife will marry a stranger, and the wife nor the new husband will receive the wealth. The wealth that the LORD gave to the man was not used for a mitzvah; therefore, the wealth turned into vanity. An example of this is a wealthy man who refuses to give any money to charity so that a poor person could be helped. It is a mitzvah to take a portion of the wealth a person is given by the LORD to help a poor person.

2. What do verses three and four refer to?

   A wealthy man who has been granted many children who is more concerned about his wealth than making a good name for himself by helping the poor have sinned. It would be better for that man not to have been born. If he were not born, he would not have sinned.[27]

---

[27] Martin McNamara et al., *The Aramaic Bible. the Targums: The Targum of Job, the Targum of Proverbs, the Targum of Qohelet*, 1991.

"The strong emphasis in the Old Testament on burial serves to bind the dead with their ancestors, and, hence, the Jews together as a people. Typical burial expressions include "he was gathered to his people" (Gen 35:29 ; 49:33) and "he rested with his fathers" (1 Kings 2:10 ; 11:43). Indeed, families were buried together (Gen 49:29-33), even if it meant traveling a great distance to do so (Gen 50:12-13). That burial resulted in the corruption of the body was understood (Gen 3:19 ; Job 17:13-16 ; Psalm 16:10 ; Acts 13:36), but it was precisely against that common recognition of the fate of the dead that the hope of resurrection was born (Isa 26:19 ; Dan 12:2)."[28]

A stillborn did not receive a funeral in ancient times. Being buried was essential to allow a person to become connected with their ancestors. Solomon said that a miserly person could not be connected to his/her ancestors because of the sin of not using the LORD's given wealth to benefit others.

3. Who are verses five and six referring?

The Sage Rashi said that these verses are referring to the rich man being described. To live two thousand years is to live twice as long as anyone who is described in the Scripture. Ultimately the rich person will die and return to the dust. Wealth cannot keep a person alive forever.[29]

---

[28] "Burial Definition and Meaning - Bible Dictionary," Bible Study Tools, accessed January 20, 2020, https://www.biblestudytools.com/dictionary/burial/.

[29] Nosson Scherman and Meir Zlotowitz, *The Book of Megillos: the Five Megillos: a New Translation with Overviews and Annotations Anthologized from the Classical Commentators* (Brooklyn, NY: Mesorah Publications, 1986).

4. What is the advantage of a wise man over a fool? (v. 8)

The knowledgeable person and foolish person both have to work for what they achieve. The difference is in how the fruits of labor are used and appreciated.[30] For example, a wise person may use his fruits to better himself and his family, while the foolish man might hold onto every fruit and not share it.

Additional notes from the Targum

In the later verses, the Targum notes that the study of the Torah will lead to an understanding of what the LORD expects people to do. The study of the Torah will also tell people how to use the gifts the LORD has given so that their toil will produce fruit that is a mitzvah to them and others.

Thoughts

What good is there to obtaining wealth that is produced from the gifts a person is given from the LORD if that wealth is not used to help others. It is a mitzvah (a blessing) to help others. Giving to charities that help others is a good use of wealth. In today's culture, one must be careful where they send their charity. There are so many instances of charities that do not help people.

An example is Good Will. Many people do not know that this organization was established to make money for its originator. Good Will at the local level does help people obtain items for a low cost. That is a fallout that occurred from the organization. A bulk of the profit made at the local level goes to pay the salary of the

---

[30] IBID.

organizer of the organization. What would the LORD say to a person who uses a mitzvah to gain wealth? According to the Scripture, that would be a violation of the LORD's Word.

Chapter Seven

Language

New American Standard 1995	Hebrew
[1] A good name is better than a good ointment, And the day of *one's* death is better than the day of one's birth.	טוֹב שֵׁם מִשֶּׁמֶן טוֹב וְיוֹם הַמָּוֶת מִיּוֹם הַוָּלְדוֹ: [2] טוֹב לָלֶכֶת אֶל־בֵּית־אֵבֶל מִלֶּכֶת אֶל־בֵּית מִשְׁתֶּה בַּאֲשֶׁר הוּא סוֹף כָּל־הָאָדָם וְהַחַי יִתֵּן אֶל־לִבּוֹ:
[2] It is better to go to a house of mourning Than to go to a house of feasting, Because that is the end of every man, And the living takes *it* to heart.	[3] טוֹב כַּעַס מִשְּׂחֹק כִּי־בְרֹעַ פָּנִים יִיטַב לֵב:
[3] Sorrow is better than laughter, For when a face is sad a heart may be happy.	[4] לֵב חֲכָמִים בְּבֵית אֵבֶל וְלֵב כְּסִילִים בְּבֵית שִׂמְחָה:
[4] The mind of the wise is in the house of mourning, While the mind of fools is in the house of pleasure.	[5] טוֹב לִשְׁמֹעַ גַּעֲרַת חָכָם מֵאִישׁ שֹׁמֵעַ שִׁיר כְּסִילִים:
[5] It is better to listen to the rebuke of a wise man Than for one to listen to the song of fools.	[6] כִּי כְקוֹל הַסִּירִים תַּחַת הַסִּיר כֵּן שְׂחֹק הַכְּסִיל וְגַם־זֶה הָבֶל:
[6] For as the crackling of thorn bushes under a pot, So is the laughter of the fool; And this too is futility.	[7] כִּי הָעֹשֶׁק יְהוֹלֵל חָכָם וִיאַבֵּד אֶת־לֵב מַתָּנָה:
[7] For oppression makes a wise man mad, And a bribe corrupts the heart.	[8] טוֹב אַחֲרִית דָּבָר מֵרֵאשִׁיתוֹ טוֹב אֶרֶךְ־רוּחַ מִגְּבַהּ־רוּחַ:
[8] The end of a matter is better than its beginning; Patience of spirit is better than haughtiness of spirit.	[9] אַל־תְּבַהֵל בְּרוּחֲךָ לִכְעוֹס כִּי כַעַס בְּחֵיק כְּסִילִים יָנוּחַ:
[9] Do not be eager in your heart to be angry, For anger resides in the bosom of fools.	[10] אַל־תֹּאמַר מֶה הָיָה שֶׁהַיָּמִים הָרִאשֹׁנִים הָיוּ טוֹבִים מֵאֵלֶּה כִּי לֹא מֵחָכְמָה שָׁאַלְתָּ עַל־זֶה:
[10] Do not say, "Why is it that the former days were better than these?" For it is not from wisdom that you ask about this.	[11] טוֹבָה חָכְמָה עִם־נַחֲלָה וְיֹתֵר לְרֹאֵי הַשָּׁמֶשׁ:
[11] Wisdom along with an inheritance is good And an advantage to those who see the sun.	[12] כִּי בְּצֵל הַחָכְמָה בְּצֵל הַכָּסֶף וְיִתְרוֹן דַּעַת הַחָכְמָה תְּחַיֶּה בְעָלֶיהָ:
	[13] רְאֵה אֶת־מַעֲשֵׂה הָאֱלֹהִים כִּי מִי יוּכַל לְתַקֵּן אֵת אֲשֶׁר עִוְּתוֹ:
	[14] בְּיוֹם טוֹבָה הֱיֵה בְטוֹב וּבְיוֹם רָעָה רְאֵה גַּם אֶת־זֶה לְעֻמַּת־זֶה עָשָׂה הָאֱלֹהִים עַל־דִּבְרַת שֶׁלֹּא יִמְצָא הָאָדָם אַחֲרָיו מְאוּמָה:
	[15] אֶת־הַכֹּל רָאִיתִי בִּימֵי הֶבְלִי יֵשׁ צַדִּיק אֹבֵד בְּצִדְקוֹ וְיֵשׁ רָשָׁע מַאֲרִיךְ בְּרָעָתוֹ:

12 For wisdom is protection *just as* money is protection, But the advantage of knowledge is that wisdom preserves the lives of its possessors.

13 Consider the work of God, For who is able to straighten what He has bent?

14 In the day of prosperity be happy, But in the day of adversity consider-- God has made the one as well as the other So that man will not discover anything *that will be* after him.

15 I have seen everything during my lifetime of futility; there is a righteous man who perishes in his righteousness and there is a wicked man who prolongs *his life* in his wickedness.

16 Do not be excessively righteous and do not be overly wise. Why should you ruin yourself?

17 Do not be excessively wicked and do not be a fool. Why should you die before your time?

18 It is good that you grasp one thing and also not let go of the other; for the one who fears God comes forth with both of them.

19 Wisdom strengthens a wise man more than ten rulers who are in a city.

20 Indeed, there is not a righteous man on earth who *continually* does good and who never sins.

21 Also, do not take seriously all words which are spoken, so that you will not hear your servant cursing you.

22 For you also have realized that you likewise have many times cursed others.

23 I tested all this with wisdom, *and* I said, "I will be wise," but it was far from me.

24 What has been is remote and exceedingly mysterious. Who can discover it?

16 אַל־תְּהִי צַדִּיק הַרְבֵּה וְאַל־תִּתְחַכַּם יוֹתֵר לָמָּה תִּשּׁוֹמֵם:

17 אַל־תִּרְשַׁע הַרְבֵּה וְאַל־תְּהִי סָכָל לָמָּה תָמוּת בְּלֹא עִתֶּךָ:

18 טוֹב אֲשֶׁר תֶּאֱחֹז בָּזֶה וְגַם־מִזֶּה אַל־תַּנַּח אֶת־יָדֶךָ כִּי־יְרֵא אֱלֹהִים יֵצֵא אֶת־כֻּלָּם:

19 הַחָכְמָה תָּעֹז לֶחָכָם מֵעֲשָׂרָה שַׁלִּיטִים אֲשֶׁר הָיוּ בָּעִיר:

20 כִּי אָדָם אֵין צַדִּיק בָּאָרֶץ אֲשֶׁר יַעֲשֶׂה־טּוֹב וְלֹא יֶחֱטָא:

21 גַּם לְכָל־הַדְּבָרִים אֲשֶׁר יְדַבֵּרוּ אַל־תִּתֵּן לִבֶּךָ אֲשֶׁר לֹא־תִשְׁמַע אֶת־עַבְדְּךָ מְקַלְלֶךָ:

22 כִּי גַּם־פְּעָמִים רַבּוֹת יָדַע לִבֶּךָ אֲשֶׁר גַּם־ (אַתְּ) [אַתָּה] קִלַּלְתָּ אֲחֵרִים:

23 כָּל־זֹה נִסִּיתִי בַחָכְמָה אָמַרְתִּי אֶחְכָּמָה וְהִיא רְחוֹקָה מִמֶּנִּי:

24 רָחוֹק מַה־שֶּׁהָיָה וְעָמֹק עָמֹק מִי יִמְצָאֶנּוּ:

25 סַבּוֹתִי אֲנִי וְלִבִּי לָדַעַת וְלָתוּר וּבַקֵּשׁ חָכְמָה וְחֶשְׁבּוֹן וְלָדַעַת רֶשַׁע כֶּסֶל וְהַסִּכְלוּת הוֹלֵלוֹת:

26 וּמוֹצֶא אֲנִי מַר מִמָּוֶת אֶת־הָאִשָּׁה אֲשֶׁר־הִיא מְצוֹדִים וַחֲרָמִים לִבָּהּ אֲסוּרִים יָדֶיהָ טוֹב לִפְנֵי הָאֱלֹהִים יִמָּלֵט מִמֶּנָּה וְחוֹטֵא יִלָּכֶד בָּהּ:

27 רְאֵה זֶה מָצָאתִי אָמְרָה קֹהֶלֶת אַחַת לְאַחַת לִמְצֹא חֶשְׁבּוֹן:

28 אֲשֶׁר עוֹד־בִּקְשָׁה נַפְשִׁי וְלֹא מָצָאתִי אָדָם אֶחָד מֵאֶלֶף מָצָאתִי וְאִשָּׁה בְכָל־אֵלֶּה לֹא מָצָאתִי:

29 לְבַד רְאֵה־זֶה מָצָאתִי אֲשֶׁר עָשָׂה הָאֱלֹהִים אֶת־הָאָדָם יָשָׁר וְהֵמָּה בִקְשׁוּ חִשְּׁבֹנוֹת רַבִּים:

25 I directed my mind to know, to investigate and to seek wisdom and an explanation, and to know the evil of folly and the foolishness of madness.
26 And I discovered more bitter than death the woman whose heart is snares and nets, whose hands are chains. One who is pleasing to God will escape from her, but the sinner will be captured by her.
27 "Behold, I have discovered this," says the Preacher, "*adding* one thing to another to find an explanation,
28 which I am still seeking but have not found. I have found one man among a thousand, but I have not found a woman among all these.
29 "Behold, I have found only this, that God made men upright, but they have sought out many devices."

Process of Discovery

Linguistics Section

Linguistic Structure

A [1] A good name is better than a good ointment, And the day of *one's* death is better than the day of one's birth. [2] It is better to go to a house of mourning Than to go to a house of feasting, Because that is the end of every man, And the living takes *it* to heart. [3] Sorrow is better than laughter, For when a face is sad a heart may be happy.

> **B** [4] The mind of the wise is in the house of mourning, While the mind of fools is in the house of pleasure. [5] It is better to listen to the rebuke of a wise man Than for one to listen to the song of fools. [6] For as the crackling of thorn bushes under a pot, So is the laughter of the fool; And this too is futility. [7] For oppression makes a wise man mad, And a bribe corrupts the heart. [8] The end of a matter is better than its beginning; Patience of spirit is better than haughtiness of spirit. [9] Do not be eager in your heart to be angry, For anger resides in the bosom of fools. [10] Do not say, "Why is it that the former days were better than these?" For it is not from wisdom that you ask about this.

> > **C** [11] Wisdom along with an inheritance is good And an advantage to those who see the sun. [12] For wisdom is protection *just as* money is protection, But the advantage of knowledge is that wisdom preserves the lives of its possessors. [13] Consider the work of God, For who is able to straighten what He has bent? [14] In the day of prosperity be happy, But in the day of adversity consider-- God has made the one as well as the other So that man will not discover anything *that will be* after him.

A' [15] I have seen everything during my lifetime of futility; there is a righteous man who perishes in his righteousness and there is a wicked man who prolongs *his life* in his wickedness. [16] Do not be excessively righteous and do not be overly wise. Why should you ruin yourself? [17] Do not be excessively wicked and do not be a fool. Why should you die before your time? [18] It is good that you grasp one thing and also not let go of the other; for the one who fears God comes forth with both of them.

B' [19] Wisdom strengthens a wise man more than ten rulers who are in a city. [20] Indeed, there is not a righteous man on earth who *continually* does good and who never sins. [21] Also, do not take seriously all words which are spoken, so that you will not hear your servant cursing you. [22] For you also have realized that you likewise have many times cursed others.

C' [23] I tested all this with wisdom, *and* I said, "I will be wise," but it was far from me. [24] What has been is remote and exceedingly mysterious. Who can discover it? [25] I directed my mind to know, to investigate and to seek wisdom and an explanation, and to know the evil of folly and the foolishness of madness. [26] And I discovered more bitter than death the woman whose heart is snares and nets, whose hands are chains. One who is pleasing to God will escape from her, but the sinner will be captured by her. [27] "Behold, I have discovered this," says the Preacher, "*adding* one thing to another to find an explanation, [28] which I am still seeking but have not found. I have found one man among a thousand, but I have not found a woman among all these. [29] "Behold, I have found only this, that God made men upright, but they have sought out many devices."

Discussion

Chapter six ended with a question. Who knows what is right for a man in life? The answer to that question is contained in this chapter.

Questioning the Passage

1. What is verse one referring to?

   This verse is the beginning of the answer to the question posed in chapter six, verse twelve. A good name is referring to a good reputation. The Sage Sforno[iv] said that an exceptional reputation is acquired by diligence and good deeds. The Sage Rashi noted that an exceptional reputation is more valuable than a valuable possession like excellent oil (ointment).[31]

The Sage Rabbi Yitzchak ben Moses Arama[v] wrote in the book title Akeidas Yitzchak, and the Sage Ibn Ezra agreed that "the man who has lived an exemplary life and acquired a good name views death as a culmination of a life well spent and as a transition to the World of Peace and Reward. Unlike the time of his birth when he is uncertain of how his life will unfold."[32]

The Targum states that the day a man dies and departs for the tomb with the right name and merits is better than the day when a wicked man is born into the world.[33]

2. How is sorrow better than laughter? (v. 3)

    The Targum states that sadness is the anger the LORD has against the righteous of the world. When the Shekinah is saddened, drought and punishment come upon the world to improve the heart of the righteous so that they will pray before the LORD that He will have mercy on them.[34]

The righteous need to remember that they may fall into the trap of sin, thus causing the Shekinah to be saddened. No one is perfect, even the righteous. Therefore, the righteous must come before the LORD in prayer, asking forgiveness for any offenses that may have been committed. It is normal for a person to sin and not even know that one sinned.

---

[31] Nosson Scherman and Meir Zlotowitz, *The Book of Megillos: the Five Megillos: a New Translation with Overviews and Annotations Anthologized from the Classical Commentators* (Brooklyn, NY: Mesorah Publications, 1986).
[32] IBID.
[33] Martin McNamara et al., *The Aramaic Bible. the Targums: The Targum of Job, the Targum of Proverbs, the Targum of Qohelet*, 1991.
[34] IBID.

3. What is verse fifteen saying about the righteous vs. the wicked?

The Sage Alshich[vi] said that the LORD causes righteous people to suffer so that they atone for any sins they may have committed so that after death, they will not be punished. The LORD allows the wicked to go unpunished so that they will have time to repent of their sins.[35] There will be evil people who never repent of their crimes and keep on sinning. On the surface, it appears that they have a more comfortable life. However, when they die, the LORD will bring a deep and lasting punishment. The righteous will go to Heaven while the wicked are sent to Hell for punishment.

4. What does it mean to be excessively righteous? (v. 16)

The Talmud gives an example of a man who would not save a woman from drowning because it is improper to look upon her.[36] In this case, it is more important to save a life than to worry about a matter of righteousness. It could be said that saving the drowning woman is more righteous than an improper look. It could be inferred that Solomon is saying that there are degrees of virtuous acts. Since there are degrees of penalties for sin as defined in Leviticus, it stands to reason that there would be degrees to righteous deeds.

5. What does the reference to the ten leaders in verse nineteen mean?

The Targum has two versions for verse nineteen. The wisdom of Joseph, son of Jacob, helped him to become wise in comparison to his ten righteous brothers who ruled in fear of the LORD. Evil inclination did not rule over them when they were in Egypt and they did not kill their brother Joseph who

---

[35] Nosson Scherman and Meir Zlotowitz, *The Book of Megillos: the Five Megillos: a New Translation with Overviews and Annotations Anthologized from the Classical Commentators* (Brooklyn, NY: Mesorah Publications, 1986).
[36] IBID.

troubled them at that time with the sound of his words. The alternate version says wisdom helps the sage to conquer his evil inclination so that he will not sin more than the strength of the ten sons of Jacob who were in the great city of Shechem when they killed every male by the sword but afterward they did not conquer their evil inclination but sold Joseph for twenty pieces of silver.

6. What does verse twenty-six mean?

This verse only applies to evil women, not all women. Wicked women use erotic techniques to trap men and have them perform evil.[37] The Targum says that one thing that is bitter to a man is when his heart is caught in the net by an angry wife. In this case, an upright man is one who divorces her with a bill of divorcement and escapes from her, but guilty before the LORD is the man who marries her and is caught in her harlotry.[38] This situation could be applied to a wife who poorly treats her husband. The husband who does not rid himself of such a wife is sinning. He must divorce her so that her evil ways do not affect his heart.

Culture Section

Discussion

People believed (and still do today) that tragic events have a meaning in life. After a tragedy, one may find that they can turn it into an advantage. For example, the story of Joseph being sold by his brothers in Genesis. If that tragedy did not occur, then when the famine hit Caanan, Joseph's family would have died and the twelve tribes of Israel would never have become a nation. Most times it takes patience

---

[37] IBID.
[38] Martin McNamara et al., *The Aramaic Bible. the Targums: The Targum of Job, the Targum of Proverbs, the Targum of Qohelet*, 1991.

and time to find the advantage from a tragedy. It should be noted that not every disaster will result in an advantage in life. Being able to turn a tragedy into an advantage is always to one's benefit.[39]

Additional Notes from the Targum

Verse two says it is better to go into the house of mourning because against all humans is the decree of death, and when a person enters a house of mourning, the righteous will repent and take to heart the matters of death. If the person has anything evil in hand, it will leave, and the evil will turn into repentance before the LORD.

Verse four says that the house of mourning is the destruction of the Temple in Jerusalem and the exile of the people to Babylon. The fools are the people who were not affected by the invasion of Babylon and are happy that they were not killed, nor was their property destroyed, nor were they taken into Exile. This is Solomon's vision the LORD gave him.

Verse five says that it is better to study the Torah and be rebuked by the teacher than it is to listen to music and have pleasure.

Verse seven says that the oppressor mocks the sage because he does not walk on his way and destroys by his evil words the wisdom of the sage's heart, which is a gift from the LORD.

The Targum adds to verse twelve that money is protected when it is used for oneself and charity.

---

[39] Rocco A. Errico and George M. Lamsa, *Aramaic Light on Ezra through the Song of Solomon* (Smyma, GA: Noohra Foundation, 2010).

Verse thirteen is referring to people who were made crocked, which is makes them lame or hunchbacked.

The Targum has two versions for verse nineteen. The wisdom of Joseph, son of Jacob, helped him to become wise in comparison to his ten righteous brothers who ruled in fear of the LORD. The evil inclination did not rule over them when they were in Egypt, and they did not kill their brother Joseph who troubled them at that time with the sound of his words. The alternate version says Wisdom helps the sage to conquer his evil inclination so that he will not sin more than the strength of the ten sons of Jacob who were in the great city of Shechem when they killed every male by the sword but afterward they did not conquer their evil inclination but sold Joseph for twenty pieces of silver.

Verse twenty-nine says that the first man, Adam, was made upright and pure. It was the serpent and Eve who seduced him to eat from the fruit of the tree. That caused the day of death to be imposed on him and the future inhabitants of the world. It is the knowledge of good and evil that is a plague upon humankind.

Thoughts

What is the most important thing to accomplish in life? According to Solomon, it is to have an exceptional reputation. To achieve this in life, the LORD offers wisdom and guidance. Wisdom can be asked for in the same way Solomon did. However, it is up to the person to act in righteous ways. The evil inclination inside of a person and the effects of Evil Inclination in the world must be avoided. It is brought out that if one's spouse is evil that the righteous person must obtain a separation or a divorce. Staying away from evil is necessary to remain righteous in the eyes of the LORD.

Chapter Eight

Language

New American Standard 1995	Hebrew
[1] Who is like the wise man and who knows the interpretation of a matter? A man's wisdom illumines him and causes his stern face to beam. [2] I say, "Keep the command of the king because of the oath before God. [3] "Do not be in a hurry to leave him. Do not join in an evil matter, for he will do whatever he pleases." [4] Since the word of the king is authoritative, who will say to him, "What are you doing?" [5] He who keeps a *royal* command experiences no trouble, for a wise heart knows the proper time and procedure. [6] For there is a proper time and procedure for every delight, though a man's trouble is heavy upon him. [7] If no one knows what will happen, who can tell him when it will happen? [8] No man has authority to restrain the wind with the wind, or authority over the day of death; and there is no discharge in the time of war, and evil will not deliver those who practice it. [9] All this I have seen and applied my mind to every deed that has been done under the sun wherein a man has exercised authority over *another* man to his hurt. [10] So then, I have seen the wicked buried, those who used to go in and out from the holy place, and they are *soon* forgotten in	מִי כְּהֶחָכָם וּמִי יוֹדֵעַ פֵּשֶׁר דָּבָר חָכְמַת אָדָם תָּאִיר פָּנָיו וְעֹז פָּנָיו יְשֻׁנֶּא: [2] אֲנִי פִּי־מֶלֶךְ שְׁמוֹר וְעַל דִּבְרַת שְׁבוּעַת אֱלֹהִים: [3] אַל־תִּבָּהֵל מִפָּנָיו תֵּלֵךְ אַל־תַּעֲמֹד בְּדָבָר רָע כִּי כָּל־אֲשֶׁר יַחְפֹּץ יַעֲשֶׂה: [4] בַּאֲשֶׁר דְּבַר־מֶלֶךְ שִׁלְטוֹן וּמִי יֹאמַר־לוֹ מַה־תַּעֲשֶׂה: [5] שׁוֹמֵר מִצְוָה לֹא יֵדַע דָּבָר רָע וְעֵת וּמִשְׁפָּט יֵדַע לֵב חָכָם: [6] כִּי לְכָל־חֵפֶץ יֵשׁ עֵת וּמִשְׁפָּט כִּי־רָעַת הָאָדָם רַבָּה עָלָיו: [7] כִּי־אֵינֶנּוּ יֹדֵעַ מַה־שֶּׁיִּהְיֶה כִּי כַּאֲשֶׁר יִהְיֶה מִי יַגִּיד לוֹ: [8] אֵין אָדָם שַׁלִּיט בָּרוּחַ לִכְלוֹא אֶת־הָרוּחַ וְאֵין שִׁלְטוֹן בְּיוֹם הַמָּוֶת וְאֵין מִשְׁלַחַת בַּמִּלְחָמָה וְלֹא־יְמַלֵּט רֶשַׁע אֶת־בְּעָלָיו: [9] אֶת־כָּל־זֶה רָאִיתִי וְנָתוֹן אֶת־לִבִּי לְכָל־מַעֲשֶׂה אֲשֶׁר נַעֲשָׂה תַּחַת הַשָּׁמֶשׁ עֵת אֲשֶׁר שָׁלַט הָאָדָם בְּאָדָם לְרַע לוֹ: [10] וּבְכֵן רָאִיתִי רְשָׁעִים קְבֻרִים וָבָאוּ וּמִמְּקוֹם קָדוֹשׁ יְהַלֵּכוּ וְיִשְׁתַּכְּחוּ בָעִיר אֲשֶׁר כֵּן־עָשׂוּ גַּם־זֶה הָבֶל: [11] אֲשֶׁר אֵין־נַעֲשָׂה פִתְגָם מַעֲשֵׂה הָרָעָה מְהֵרָה עַל־כֵּן מָלֵא לֵב בְּנֵי־הָאָדָם בָּהֶם לַעֲשׂוֹת רָע: [12] אֲשֶׁר חֹטֶא עֹשֶׂה רָע מְאַת וּמַאֲרִיךְ לוֹ כִּי גַּם־יוֹדֵעַ אָנִי אֲשֶׁר יִהְיֶה־טּוֹב לְיִרְאֵי הָאֱלֹהִים אֲשֶׁר יִירְאוּ מִלְּפָנָיו: [13] וְטוֹב לֹא־יִהְיֶה לָרָשָׁע וְלֹא־יַאֲרִיךְ יָמִים כַּצֵּל אֲשֶׁר אֵינֶנּוּ יָרֵא מִלִּפְנֵי אֱלֹהִים: [14] יֶשׁ־הֶבֶל אֲשֶׁר נַעֲשָׂה עַל־הָאָרֶץ אֲשֶׁר יֵשׁ צַדִּיקִים אֲשֶׁר מַגִּיעַ אֲלֵהֶם כְּמַעֲשֵׂה הָרְשָׁעִים

the city where they did thus. This too is futility.

[11] Because the sentence against an evil deed is not executed quickly, therefore the hearts of the sons of men among them are given fully to do evil.

[12] Although a sinner does evil a hundred *times* and may lengthen his *life*, still I know that it will be well for those who fear God, who fear Him openly.

[13] But it will not be well for the evil man and he will not lengthen his days like a shadow, because he does not fear God.

[14] There is futility which is done on the earth, that is, there are righteous men to whom it happens according to the deeds of the wicked. On the other hand, there are evil men to whom it happens according to the deeds of the righteous. I say that this too is futility.

[15] So I commended pleasure, for there is nothing good for a man under the sun except to eat and to drink and to be merry, and this will stand by him in his toils *throughout* the days of his life which God has given him under the sun.

[16] When I gave my heart to know wisdom and to see the task which has been done on the earth e*ven though one should never sleep day or night),

[17] and I saw every work of God, *I concluded* that man cannot discover the work which has been done under the sun. Even though man should seek laboriously, he will not discover; and though the wise man should say, "I know," he cannot discover.

וְיֵשׁ רְשָׁעִים שֶׁמַּגִּיעַ אֲלֵהֶם כְּמַעֲשֵׂה הַצַּדִּיקִים אָמַרְתִּי שֶׁגַּם־זֶה הָבֶל:

[15] וְשִׁבַּחְתִּי אֲנִי אֶת־הַשִּׂמְחָה אֲשֶׁר אֵין־טוֹב לָאָדָם תַּחַת הַשֶּׁמֶשׁ כִּי אִם־לֶאֱכוֹל וְלִשְׁתּוֹת וְלִשְׂמוֹחַ וְהוּא יִלְוֶנּוּ בַעֲמָלוֹ יְמֵי חַיָּיו אֲשֶׁר־נָתַן־לוֹ הָאֱלֹהִים תַּחַת הַשָּׁמֶשׁ:

[16] כַּאֲשֶׁר נָתַתִּי אֶת־לִבִּי לָדַעַת חָכְמָה וְלִרְאוֹת אֶת־הָעִנְיָן אֲשֶׁר נַעֲשָׂה עַל־הָאָרֶץ כִּי גַם בַּיּוֹם וּבַלַּיְלָה שֵׁנָה בְּעֵינָיו אֵינֶנּוּ רֹאֶה:

[17] וְרָאִיתִי אֶת־כָּל־מַעֲשֵׂה הָאֱלֹהִים כִּי לֹא יוּכַל הָאָדָם לִמְצוֹא אֶת־הַמַּעֲשֶׂה אֲשֶׁר נַעֲשָׂה תַחַת־הַשֶּׁמֶשׁ בְּשֶׁל אֲשֶׁר יַעֲמֹל הָאָדָם לְבַקֵּשׁ וְלֹא יִמְצָא וְגַם אִם־יֹאמַר הֶחָכָם לָדַעַת לֹא יוּכַל לִמְצֹא:

Process of Discovery

Linguistics Section

Linguistic Structure

[Wisdom about authority] [1] Who is like the wise man and who knows the interpretation of a matter? A man's wisdom illumines him and causes his stern face to beam. [2] I say, "Keep the command of the king because of the oath before God. [3] "Do not be in a hurry to leave him. Do not join in an evil matter, for he will do whatever he pleases." [4] Since the word of the king is authoritative, who will say to him, "What are you doing?" [5] He who keeps a *royal* command experiences no trouble, for a wise heart knows the proper time and procedure. [6] For there is a proper time and procedure for every delight, though a man's trouble is heavy upon him. [7] If no one knows what will happen, who can tell him when it will happen? [8] No man has authority to restrain the wind with the wind, or authority over the day of death; and there is no discharge in the time of war, and evil will not deliver those who practice it.

A [9] All this I have seen and applied my mind to every deed that has been done under the sun wherein a man has exercised authority over *another* man to his hurt. [10] So then, I have seen the wicked buried, those who used to go in and out from the holy place, and they are *soon* forgotten in the city where they did thus. This too is futility. [11] Because the sentence against an evil deed is not executed quickly, therefore the hearts of the sons of men among them are given fully to do evil.

> **B** [12] Although a sinner does evil a hundred *times* and may lengthen his *life*, still I know that it will be well for those who fear God, who fear Him openly. [13] But it will not be well for the evil man and he will not lengthen his days like a shadow, because he does not fear God.

A' [14] There is futility which is done on the earth, that is, there are righteous men to whom it happens according to the deeds of the wicked. On the other hand, there are evil men to whom it happens according to the deeds of the righteous. I say that this too is futility. [15] So I commended pleasure, for there is nothing good for a man under the sun except to eat and to drink and to be merry, and this will stand by him in his toils *throughout* the days of his life which God has given him under the sun.

[Seek wisdom] [16] When I gave my heart to know wisdom and to see the task which has been done on the earth even though one should never sleep day or night), [17] and I saw every work of God, *I concluded* that man cannot discover the work which has been done under the sun. Even though man should seek laboriously, he will not discover; and though the wise man should say, "I know," he cannot discover.

Discussion

The short chiasm in the middle of the chapter speaks about wicked people and why reverence must be given to the LORD.

Questioning the Passage

1. Who is the King in verse two?

    The Sage Rashi said that the king is the LORD. The commandment of the King is from the oath that Israel took at Mount Sinai when the LORD gave them the Torah. There is an additional view that the earthly King's commandments must be obeyed as long as the commandment does not violate any part of the LORD's Torah.[40]

2. What does the reference "day of death" mean in verse eight?

    According to the Midrash, this means that a person cannot say to the Angel of Death, "Wait for Me until I finish my business and then I will come."[41] The Angel of Death will come to visit each human when it is their time to leave the Earth. A person does not have control over when this visit will occur. Besides, no one can tell the Angel of Death that they are not ready to leave. They will go with the angel.

---

[40] Rocco A. Errico and George M. Lamsa, *Aramaic Light on Ezra through the Song of Solomon* (Smyma, GA: Noohra Foundation, 2010).

[41] Nosson Scherman and Meir Zlotowitz, *The Book of Megillos: the Five Megillos: a New Translation with Overviews and Annotations Anthologized from the Classical Commentators* (Brooklyn, NY: Mesorah Publications, 1986).

3. What does verse eleven mean?

Most of the time, evil deeds are not punished immediately; therefore, persons tend to do more evil. The evil deeds are not ones that break the laws of the government but rather are the rules of the LORD. For many wicked people, they stay within the law of their government but commit sins according to the Torah. The LORD does not execute punishment upon them immediately so they can repent. Eventually, they will have to answer for their evil. Verse ten says that these wicked people and their evil acts are soon forgotten after their death because of the knowledge that the LORD will not accept them into Heaven because of their evil.

Culture Section

Discussion

In the Middle East, people rejoice to hear the words of a wise person. They respect their counsel and advice. A smart person is humble and lovable. It is said that wisdom makes their faces shine.[42]

Immortality was in its infancy in the days of Solomon. Very few people thought that there was an afterlife. Life was very uncertain because of the conditions of human existence and the constant threat of war. Therefore, kings, princes, and rich people tried to make the best of their lives. A slogan was, "today we eat, drink, and be merry because we shall die." For these rich men, they discovered that this type of existence became boring.[43] Solomon said that there must be more to life than just eating and drinking. There has to be a higher purpose from the LORD for our lives. It is each person's task to discover how they can contribute to society.

---

[42] Rocco A. Errico and George M. Lamsa, *Aramaic Light on Ezra through the Song of Solomon* (Smyma, GA: Noohra Foundation, 2010).

[43] IBID.

Additional notes from the Targum

Verse three says that when the LORD becomes angry, do not cease praying before Him. It is better to come quickly before the LORD to seek mercy so that one will not be convicted of unrepentant evil.

The Targum views the opening verses as referring to the LORD and not to an earthly king.

The Targum verse six states that there is a time for good and evil. By true justice, the whole world will be judged and when it is decreed by the LORD that there will be punishments in the world on account of the sin of the people who do evil which is against Him. This sentence says that the LORD knows that there are times upon the earth when evil and sin rage uncontrolled. The LORD then sent His messengers to tell the people to come back to the LORD. When they did not stop their evil ways, it became time to punish the world. After Solomon's reign, Israel fell into periods of evil and good. Eventually, the evil became more potent than the good and the LORD had no choice but to step in. He brought the Babylonians from the north to punish Judea, to destroy Jerusalem and the Temple of the LORD.

Thoughts

Humans will never fully comprehend the ways of the LORD. It does not matter how many prophets the LORD sends to us; there will always be mysteries that are not within our reach. Even the LORD's Messiah was not able to tell us everything that humans wanted to know about how the world works. There are times when people have to accept the way things are. Humans have been able over time to change the landscape of life to make things better. Unfortunately, there will always be people who do not use their gifts and talents from the LORD to better themselves or society.

There will always be wicked people who take advantage of others. There will always be self-centered people who will ensure that their life is the best no matter what suffering they may cause. What can people do? To live by the commandments of the LORD through the Scripture is the best way to become and remain righteous.

Chapter Nine

Language

New American Standard 1995	Hebrew
[1] For I have taken all this to my heart and explain it that righteous men, wise men, and their deeds are in the hand of God. Man does not know whether *it will be* love or hatred; anything awaits him. [2] It is the same for all. There is one fate for the righteous and for the wicked; for the good, for the clean and for the unclean; for the man who offers a sacrifice and for the one who does not sacrifice. As the good man is, so is the sinner; as the swearer is, so is the one who is afraid to swear. [3] This is an evil in all that is done under the sun, that there is one fate for all men. Furthermore, the hearts of the sons of men are full of evil and insanity is in their hearts throughout their lives. Afterwards they *go* to the dead. [4] For whoever is joined with all the living, there is hope; surely a live dog is better than a dead lion. [5] For the living know they will die; but the dead do not know anything, nor have they any longer a reward, for their memory is forgotten. [6] Indeed their love, their hate and their zeal have already perished, and they will no longer have a share in all that is done under the sun. [7] Go *then*, eat your bread in happiness and drink your wine with a cheerful heart; for God has already approved your works.	כִּי אֶת־כָּל־זֶה נָתַתִּי אֶל־לִבִּי וְלָבוּר אֶת־כָּל־זֶה אֲשֶׁר הַצַּדִּיקִים וְהַחֲכָמִים וַעֲבָדֵיהֶם בְּיַד הָאֱלֹהִים גַּם־אַהֲבָה גַם־שִׂנְאָה אֵין יוֹדֵעַ הָאָדָם הַכֹּל לִפְנֵיהֶם: [2] הַכֹּל כַּאֲשֶׁר לַכֹּל מִקְרֶה אֶחָד לַצַּדִּיק וְלָרָשָׁע לַטּוֹב וְלַטָּהוֹר וְלַטָּמֵא וְלַזֹּבֵחַ וְלַאֲשֶׁר אֵינֶנּוּ זֹבֵחַ כַּטּוֹב כַּחֹטָא הַנִּשְׁבָּע כַּאֲשֶׁר שְׁבוּעָה יָרֵא: [3] זֶה רָע בְּכֹל אֲשֶׁר־נַעֲשָׂה תַּחַת הַשֶּׁמֶשׁ כִּי־מִקְרֶה אֶחָד לַכֹּל וְגַם לֵב בְּנֵי־הָאָדָם מָלֵא־רָע וְהוֹלֵלוֹת בִּלְבָבָם בְּחַיֵּיהֶם וְאַחֲרָיו אֶל־הַמֵּתִים: [4] כִּי־מִי אֲשֶׁר (יְבֻחַר) [יְחֻבַּר] אֶל כָּל־הַחַיִּים יֵשׁ בִּטָּחוֹן כִּי־לְכֶלֶב חַי הוּא טוֹב מִן־הָאַרְיֵה הַמֵּת: [5] כִּי הַחַיִּים יוֹדְעִים שֶׁיָּמֻתוּ וְהַמֵּתִים אֵינָם יוֹדְעִים מְאוּמָה וְאֵין־עוֹד לָהֶם שָׂכָר כִּי נִשְׁכַּח זִכְרָם: [6] גַּם אַהֲבָתָם גַּם־שִׂנְאָתָם גַּם־קִנְאָתָם כְּבָר אָבָדָה וְחֵלֶק אֵין־לָהֶם עוֹד לְעוֹלָם בְּכֹל אֲשֶׁר־נַעֲשָׂה תַּחַת הַשָּׁמֶשׁ: [7] לֵךְ אֱכֹל בְּשִׂמְחָה לַחְמֶךָ וּשְׁתֵה בְלֶב־טוֹב יֵינֶךָ כִּי כְבָר רָצָה הָאֱלֹהִים אֶת־מַעֲשֶׂיךָ: [8] בְּכָל־עֵת יִהְיוּ בְגָדֶיךָ לְבָנִים וְשֶׁמֶן עַל־רֹאשְׁךָ אַל־יֶחְסָר: [9] רְאֵה חַיִּים עִם־אִשָּׁה אֲשֶׁר־אָהַבְתָּ כָּל־יְמֵי חַיֵּי הֶבְלֶךָ אֲשֶׁר נָתַן־לְךָ תַּחַת הַשֶּׁמֶשׁ כֹּל יְמֵי הֶבְלֶךָ כִּי הוּא חֶלְקְךָ בַּחַיִּים וּבַעֲמָלְךָ אֲשֶׁר־אַתָּה עָמֵל תַּחַת הַשָּׁמֶשׁ: [10] כֹּל אֲשֶׁר תִּמְצָא יָדְךָ לַעֲשׂוֹת בְּכֹחֲךָ עֲשֵׂה כִּי אֵין מַעֲשֶׂה וְחֶשְׁבּוֹן וְדַעַת וְחָכְמָה בִּשְׁאוֹל אֲשֶׁר אַתָּה הֹלֵךְ שָׁמָּה: ס [11] שַׁבְתִּי וְרָאֹה תַחַת־הַשֶּׁמֶשׁ כִּי לֹא לַקַּלִּים הַמֵּרוֹץ וְלֹא לַגִּבּוֹרִים הַמִּלְחָמָה וְגַם לֹא

^{8} Let your clothes be white all the time, and let not oil be lacking on your head.

^{9} Enjoy life with the woman whom you love all the days of your fleeting life which He has given to you under the sun; for this is your reward in life and in your toil in which you have labored under the sun.

^{10} Whatever your hand finds to do, do *it* with *all* your might; for there is no activity or planning or knowledge or wisdom in Sheol where you are going.

^{11} I again saw under the sun that the race is not to the swift and the battle is not to the warriors, and neither is bread to the wise nor wealth to the discerning nor favor to men of ability; for time and chance overtake them all.

^{12} Moreover, man does not know his time: like fish caught in a treacherous net and birds trapped in a snare, so the sons of men are ensnared at an evil time when it suddenly falls on them.

^{13} Also this I came to see as wisdom under the sun, and it impressed me.

^{14} There was a small city with few men in it and a great king came to it, surrounded it and constructed large siegeworks against it.

^{15} But there was found in it a poor wise man and he delivered the city by his wisdom. Yet no one remembered that poor man.

^{16} So I said, "Wisdom is better than strength." But the wisdom of the poor man is despised and his words are not heeded.

^{17} The words of the wise heard in quietness are *better* than the shouting of a ruler among fools.

^{18} Wisdom is better than weapons of war, but one sinner destroys much good.

לַחֲכָמִים לֶחֶם וְגַם לֹא לַנְּבֹנִים עֹשֶׁר וְגַם לֹא
לַיֹּדְעִים חֵן כִּי־עֵת וָפֶגַע יִקְרֶה אֶת־כֻּלָּם:
12 כִּי גַּם לֹא־יֵדַע הָאָדָם אֶת־עִתּוֹ כַּדָּגִים
שֶׁנֶּאֱחָזִים בִּמְצוֹדָה רָעָה וְכַצִּפֳּרִים הָאֲחֻזוֹת
בַּפָּח כָּהֵם יוּקָשִׁים בְּנֵי הָאָדָם לְעֵת רָעָה
כְּשֶׁתִּפּוֹל עֲלֵיהֶם פִּתְאֹם:
13 גַּם־זֹה רָאִיתִי חָכְמָה תַּחַת הַשָּׁמֶשׁ
וּגְדוֹלָה הִיא אֵלָי:
14 עִיר קְטַנָּה וַאֲנָשִׁים בָּהּ מְעָט וּבָא־אֵלֶיהָ
מֶלֶךְ גָּדוֹל וְסָבַב אֹתָהּ וּבָנָה עָלֶיהָ מְצוֹדִים
גְּדֹלִים:
15 וּמָצָא בָהּ אִישׁ מִסְכֵּן חָכָם וּמִלַּט־הוּא
אֶת־הָעִיר בְּחָכְמָתוֹ וְאָדָם לֹא זָכַר אֶת־
הָאִישׁ הַמִּסְכֵּן הַהוּא:
16 וְאָמַרְתִּי אָנִי טוֹבָה חָכְמָה מִגְּבוּרָה
וְחָכְמַת הַמִּסְכֵּן בְּזוּיָה וּדְבָרָיו אֵינָם נִשְׁמָעִים:
17 דִּבְרֵי חֲכָמִים בְּנַחַת נִשְׁמָעִים מִזַּעֲקַת
מוֹשֵׁל בַּכְּסִילִים:
18 טוֹבָה חָכְמָה מִכְּלֵי קְרָב וְחוֹטֶא אֶחָד
יְאַבֵּד טוֹבָה הַרְבֵּה:

Process of Discovery

Linguistics Section

Linguistic Structure

A[1] For I have taken all this to my heart and explain it that righteous men, wise men, and their deeds are in the hand of God. Man does not know whether *it will be* love or hatred; anything awaits him.

> **B1** [2] It is the same for all. There is one fate for the righteous and for the wicked; for the good, for the clean and for the unclean; for the man who offers a sacrifice and for the one who does not sacrifice. As the good man is, so is the sinner; as the swearer is, so is the one who is afraid to swear.

> **B2** [3] This is an evil in all that is done under the sun, that there is one fate for all men. Furthermore, the hearts of the sons of men are full of evil and insanity is in their hearts throughout their lives. Afterwards they *go* to the dead.

> **B3** [4] For whoever is joined with all the living, there is hope; surely a live dog is better than a dead lion. [5] For the living know they will die; but the dead do not know anything, nor have they any longer a reward, for their memory is forgotten.

A' [6] Indeed their love, their hate and their zeal have already perished, and they will no longer have a share in all that is done under the sun.

[Do not worry, be happy] [7] Go *then*, eat your bread in happiness and drink your wine with a cheerful heart; for God has already approved your works. [8] Let your clothes be white all the time, and let not oil be lacking on your head. [9] Enjoy life with the woman whom you love all the days of your fleeting life which He has given to you under the sun; for this is your reward in life and in your toil in which you have labored under the sun. [10] Whatever your hand finds to do, do *it* with *all* your might; for there is no activity or planning or knowledge or wisdom in Sheol where you are going.

A [11] I again saw under the sun that the race is not to the swift and the battle is not to the warriors, and neither is bread to the wise nor wealth to the discerning nor favor to men of ability; for time and chance overtake them all.

B [12] Moreover, man does not know his time: like fish caught in a treacherous net and birds trapped in a snare, so the sons of men are ensnared at an evil time when it suddenly falls on them.

A' [13] Also this I came to see as wisdom under the sun, and it impressed me.

[Allegory] [14] There was a small city with few men in it and a great king came to it, surrounded it and constructed large siegeworks against it. [15] But there was found in it a poor wise man and he delivered the city by his wisdom. Yet no one remembered that poor man. [16] So I said, "Wisdom is better than strength." But the wisdom of the poor man is despised and his words are not heeded.

[Wisdom] [17] The words of the wise heard in quietness are *better* than the shouting of a ruler among fools. [18] Wisdom is better than weapons of war, but one sinner destroys much good.

Discussion

This chapter consists of two short chiasms and two sayings. The chiasms and the saying do work together to bring out the point that the wise and wicked both end up in the same situation at the end of their lives. The idea of the wise and wicked being separated was developed in the previous chapter.

Questioning the Passage

1. What is the final fate for all people? (v. 2)

   The Sage Rashi said that everyone knows that death is the universal equalizer that awaits every human. The wise person chooses to take the proper path because the person realizes that there is a distinction between good and evil in the Hereafter.[44]

During the time of Solomon, the idea of a Hereafter was in its infancy. This idea can be seen in this verse and similar verses. It is possible that some redacting was done to this chapter, and others, which go into the idea of the world to come since the idea of an afterlife was not fully understood.

2. What is the main point of verse three?
    The Sage Metzudas David[vii] said that the same fate, death, awaits for the wise and the wicked. What the wise and righteous people have to believe is that there is a time when justice will be given to those who were wicked or evil in this world.

    The Targum adds that an evil providence exists in the world, which does infect humans.

3. What does "I saw under the sun…" in verse eleven mean?
    The Sage Rashi said that this verse and next are Solomon's affirmation of his principles that this world is transitory, and the LORD governs man.[45] The Targum adds that Solomon observed that there are men as swift as eagles, but they do not escape death. An intelligent person cannot escape death caused by famine. A wealthy person may not know to find mercy in the eyes of his/her king.

---

[44] Nosson Scherman and Meir Zlotowitz, *The Book of Megillos: the Five Megillos: a New Translation with Overviews and Annotations Anthologized from the Classical Commentators* (Brooklyn, NY: Mesorah Publications, 1986).
[45] IBID

Verse twelve continues that a person does not know when their time on the Earth is finished in the same way that a fish does not know when it will be caught in a net.

4. What does the allegory of verses 14-16 mean?

    The Sage Rashi and Ibn Ezra said that this allegory is referring to the wisdom of a poor man who is despised, deprecated, and ignored. In an emergency, the wise person can accomplish more than the mighty, as illustrated by this allegory. It was wisdom and not esteem that saved the whole town from the might of the attacker.[46]

Culture Section

Discussion

Garments made of white material symbolized honesty and piety. The King and his court generally wore white.[47]

Oil was symbolic of the light of the LORD and wealth. Wealthy people would anoint themselves daily with oil.[48]

Additional Notes from the Targum

The Targum adds to verse four, who is the man who adheres to all the words of the Torah and has the hope to acquire the life of the world to come.

---

[46] IBID

[47] Rocco A. Errico and George M. Lamsa, *Aramaic Light on Ezra through the Song of Solomon* (Smyma, GA: Noohra Foundation, 2010).

[48] IBID.

The Targum adds to verse six that there are wicked people who never make a positive contribution to the world

Thoughts

People need to accept that it is by their actions of righteousness or evil that determines the course of the world. Today people like to blame everyone else for the woes of the world. The evil that exists in the world is caused by greedy people who want wealth and prestige for themselves at the cost of others. These types of people like to blame everyone else for the difficulties of the world and even for their actions. Solomon says that people need to fess up and accept responsibility for their actions. It is better to use wisdom to help others and to raise oneself into a position of righteousness then to be wicked This act is not done by the LORD but by the individual.

Language

New American Standard 1995	Hebrew
¹ Dead flies make a perfumer's oil stink, so a little foolishness is weightier than wisdom *and* honor. ² A wise man's heart *directs him* toward the right, but the foolish man's heart *directs him* toward the left. ³ Even when the fool walks along the road, his sense is lacking and he demonstrates to everyone *that* he is a fool. ⁴ If the ruler's temper rises against you, do not abandon your position, because composure allays great offenses. ⁵ There is an evil I have seen under the sun, like an error which goes forth from the ruler-- ⁶ folly is set in many exalted places while rich men sit in humble places. ⁷ I have seen slaves *riding* on horses and princes walking like slaves on the land. ⁸ He who digs a pit may fall into it, and a serpent may bite him who breaks through a wall. ⁹ He who quarries stones may be hurt by them, and he who splits logs may be endangered by them. ¹⁰ If the axe is dull and he does not sharpen *its* edge, then he must exert more strength. Wisdom has the advantage of giving success. ¹¹ If the serpent bites before being charmed, there is no profit for the charmer. ¹² Words from the mouth of a wise man are gracious, while the lips of a fool consume him;	זְבוּבֵי מָוֶת יַבְאִישׁ יַבִּיעַ שֶׁמֶן רוֹקֵחַ יָקָר מֵחָכְמָה מִכָּבוֹד סִכְלוּת מְעָט: ² לֵב חָכָם לִימִינוֹ וְלֵב כְּסִיל לִשְׂמֹאלוֹ: ³ וְגַם־בַּדֶּרֶךְ (כְּשֶׁהַסָּכָל) [כְּשֶׁסָּכָל] הֹלֵךְ לִבּוֹ חָסֵר וְאָמַר לַכֹּל סָכָל הוּא: ⁴ אִם־רוּחַ הַמּוֹשֵׁל תַּעֲלֶה עָלֶיךָ מְקוֹמְךָ אַל־תַּנַּח כִּי מַרְפֵּא יַנִּיחַ חֲטָאִים גְּדוֹלִים: ⁵ יֵשׁ רָעָה רָאִיתִי תַּחַת הַשָּׁמֶשׁ כִּשְׁגָגָה שֶׁיֹּצָא מִלִּפְנֵי הַשַּׁלִּיט: ⁶ נִתַּן הַסֶּכֶל בַּמְּרוֹמִים רַבִּים וַעֲשִׁירִים בַּשֵּׁפֶל יֵשֵׁבוּ: ⁷ רָאִיתִי עֲבָדִים עַל־סוּסִים וְשָׂרִים הֹלְכִים כַּעֲבָדִים עַל־הָאָרֶץ: ⁸ חֹפֵר גּוּמָּץ בּוֹ יִפּוֹל וּפֹרֵץ גָּדֵר יִשְּׁכֶנּוּ נָחָשׁ: ⁹ מַסִּיעַ אֲבָנִים יֵעָצֵב בָּהֶם בּוֹקֵעַ עֵצִים יִסָּכֶן בָּם: ¹⁰ אִם־קֵהָה הַבַּרְזֶל וְהוּא לֹא־פָנִים קִלְקַל וַחֲיָלִים יְגַבֵּר וְיִתְרוֹן (הַכְשֵׁיר) [הַכְשֵׁר] חָכְמָה: ¹¹ אִם־יִשֹּׁךְ הַנָּחָשׁ בְּלוֹא־לָחַשׁ וְאֵין יִתְרוֹן לְבַעַל הַלָּשׁוֹן: ¹² דִּבְרֵי פִי־חָכָם חֵן וְשִׂפְתוֹת כְּסִיל תְּבַלְּעֶנּוּ: ¹³ תְּחִלַּת דִּבְרֵי־פִיהוּ סִכְלוּת וְאַחֲרִית פִּיהוּ הוֹלֵלוּת רָעָה: ¹⁴ וְהַסָּכָל יַרְבֶּה דְבָרִים לֹא־יֵדַע הָאָדָם מַה־שֶׁיִּהְיֶה וַאֲשֶׁר יִהְיֶה מֵאַחֲרָיו מִי יַגִּיד לוֹ: ¹⁵ עֲמַל הַכְּסִילִים תְּיַגְּעֶנּוּ אֲשֶׁר לֹא־יָדַע לָלֶכֶת אֶל־עִיר: ¹⁶ אִי־לָךְ אֶרֶץ שֶׁמַּלְכֵּךְ נָעַר וְשָׂרַיִךְ בַּבֹּקֶר יֹאכֵלוּ: ¹⁷ אַשְׁרֵיךְ אֶרֶץ שֶׁמַּלְכֵּךְ בֶּן־חוֹרִים וְשָׂרַיִךְ בָּעֵת יֹאכֵלוּ בִּגְבוּרָה וְלֹא בַשְּׁתִי: ¹⁸ בַּעֲצַלְתַּיִם יִמַּךְ הַמְּקָרֶה וּבְשִׁפְלוּת יָדַיִם יִדְלֹף הַבָּיִת:

לִשְׂחוֹק֙ עֹשִׂ֣ים לֶ֔חֶם וְיַ֖יִן יְשַׂמַּ֣ח חַיִּ֑ים [19]
וְהַכֶּ֖סֶף יַעֲנֶ֥ה אֶת־הַכֹּֽל:
גַּ֣ם בְּמַדָּֽעֲךָ֙ מֶ֣לֶךְ אַל־תְּקַלֵּ֔ל וּבְחַדְרֵי֙ [20]
מִשְׁכָּ֣בְךָ֔ אַל־תְּקַלֵּ֖ל עָשִׁ֑יר כִּ֣י ע֤וֹף הַשָּׁמַ֨יִם֙
יוֹלִ֣יךְ אֶת־הַקּ֔וֹל וּבַ֥עַל (הַכְּנָפַ֖יִם) [כְּנָפַ֖יִם]
יַגֵּ֥יד דָּבָֽר:

13 the beginning of his talking is folly and the end of it is wicked madness.

14 Yet the fool multiplies words. No man knows what will happen, and who can tell him what will come after him?

15 The toil of a fool *so* wearies him that he does not *even* know how to go to a city.

16 Woe to you, O land, whose king is a lad and whose princes feast in the morning.

17 Blessed are you, O land, whose king is of nobility and whose princes eat at the appropriate time-- for strength and not for drunkenness.

18 Through indolence the rafters sag, and through slackness the house leaks.

19 *Men* prepare a meal for enjoyment, and wine makes life merry, and money is the answer to everything.

20 Furthermore, in your bedchamber do not curse a king, and in your sleeping rooms do not curse a rich man, for a bird of the heavens will carry the sound and the winged creature will make the matter known.

Process of Discovery

Linguistics Section

Linguistic Structure

[1] Dead flies make a perfumer's oil stink, so a little foolishness is weightier than wisdom *and* honor.

[2] A wise man's heart *directs him* toward the right, but the foolish man's heart *directs him* toward the left.

[3] Even when the fool walks along the road, his sense is lacking and he demonstrates to everyone *that* he is a fool.

[4] If the ruler's temper rises against you, do not abandon your position, because composure allays great offenses.

[5] There is an evil I have seen under the sun, like an error which goes forth from the ruler-- [6] folly is set in many exalted places while rich men sit in humble places.

[7] I have seen slaves *riding* on horses and princes walking like slaves on the land.

[8] He who digs a pit may fall into it, and a serpent may bite him who breaks through a wall.

[9] He who quarries stones may be hurt by them, and he who splits logs may be endangered by them. [10] If the axe is dull and he does not sharpen *its* edge, then he must exert more strength. Wisdom has the advantage of giving success.

[11] If the serpent bites before being charmed, there is no profit for the charmer.

[12] Words from the mouth of a wise man are gracious, while the lips of a fool consume him; [13] the beginning of his talking is folly, and the end of it is wicked madness. [14] Yet

the fool multiplies words. No man knows what will happen, and who can tell him what will come after him?

[15] The toil of a fool *so* wearies him that he does not *even* know how to go to a city.

[16] Woe to you, O land, whose king is a lad and whose princes feast in the morning.

[17] Blessed are you, O land, whose king is of nobility and whose princes eat at the appropriate time-- for strength and not for drunkenness.

[18] Through indolence the rafters sag, and through slackness the house leaks.

[19] *Men* prepare a meal for enjoyment, and wine makes life merry, and money is the answer to everything.

[20] Furthermore, in your bedchamber do not curse a king, and in your sleeping rooms do not curse a rich man, for a bird of the heavens will carry the sound and the winged creature will make the matter known.

Discussion

This chapter is a collection of sayings from King Solomon.

The Proverbs of the chapter

1. Dead flies make a perfumer's oil stink, so a little foolishness is weightier than wisdom *and* honor.

    Family, friends, and admirers can quickly notice one mistake. Wisdom and knowledge are like perfume in that they must be kept secure and for future generations.[49]

2. A wise man's heart *directs him* toward the right, but the foolish man's heart *directs him* toward the left.

    The heart of a sage is to seek the Torah and its wisdom, which is given by the right hand of the LORD, while a fool sets out to acquire gold and silver.[50]

3. Even when the fool walks along the road, his sense is lacking and he demonstrates to everyone *that* he is a fool.

    When a fool walks in a rebellious path, his heart is lacking wisdom and does things that are not right to be done.[51] Solomon is calling not following the Torah as being on the rebellious path. When a person does not support the Word of the LORD, the individual will commit sins against the LORD. It is better to stay on the path of righteousness as prescribed by the Torah.

---

[49] Rocco A. Errico and George M. Lamsa, *Aramaic Light on Ezra through the Song of Solomon* (Smyma, GA: Noohra Foundation, 2010)..

[50] Martin McNamara et al., *The Aramaic Bible. the Targums: The Targum of Job, the Targum of Proverbs, the Targum of Qohelet*, 1991.

[51] IBID.

4. If the ruler's temper rises against you, do not abandon your position, because composure allays great offenses.

> The ruler's temper is Evil Inclination. If a person is infected with Evil Inclination, the individual will be drawn into sin and evil. The cure for this infection is the words of the Torah. When a sinful person turns to life under the Torah, his/her sins are forgiven and forgotten by the LORD.[52]

5. [5] There is an evil I have seen under the sun, like an error which goes forth from the ruler-- [6] folly is set in many exalted places while rich men sit in humble places.

> Solomon saw an evil that existed on Earth that caused damage in the world. The LORD enabled wicked and the foolish Edom to enjoy good luck and to enjoy prosperity from the highest heavens, and his armies were proud and numerous while the people of Israel were enslaved under Edom in exile. Edom's various sins, the rich in property became poor and Edom became a lowly state among the nations of the world.[53]

6. I have seen slaves *riding* on horses and princes walking like slaves on the land. This is a prophecy of Solomon. He saw the people who were enslaved to Israel growing strong and riding on horses like rulers while the people and nobles of Israel walked like slaves on the ground.[54] This prophecy would come to pass when the nations that surrounded Judah were able to take advantage of the Babylonian invasion. These nations were once subservient to Israel during the days of David and Solomon. The tables had turned

---

[52] IBID.
[53] IBID.
[54] IBID.

when the Babylonians invaded. Those nations plundered Israel while Israel's elite and nobles walked as slaves to the Babylonian capital.

7. He who digs a pit may fall into it, and a serpent may bite him who breaks through a wall.

    The Israelites caused this problem of being enslaved by Babylon. A man who digs a pit at a crossroads is liable to fall in it, so the people who transgressed against the LORD fell into the hands of a wicked king.[55]

8. He who quarries stones may be hurt by them, and he who splits logs may be endangered by them. [10] If the axe is dull and he does not sharpen *its* edge, then he must exert more strength. Wisdom has the advantage of giving success.

    Solomon the prophet, said that the son of Hezekiah would sin and worship images of stone. Therefore, the LORD will deliver him into the hands of the Assyrians. The Words of the LORD were initially given to the people on stone tablets. The laws on the tablets should have been obeyed.

    Rabshakeh, his brother, worshiped images of wood and forsake the words of the Torah which was stored in acacia wood. Therefore, he will be burned, like wood, by an angel of the LORD.

    When the people of Israel sinned, the heavens became hard as iron and rain did not fall upon the earth. This sin caused a famine which destroyed the world. When the people repented of their sins and prevailed over evil

---

[55] IBID.

inclination and offered a prayer to the LORD, He forgave them. The LORD then opened the heavens to them (it rained).[56]

9. If the serpent bites before being charmed, there is no profit for the charmer. The serpent will come to stir up harm and trouble in the world when Israel sins and does not occupy herself with the words of the Torah quietly. Also, there is no advantage for a slanderer who speaks with a third tongue, for he will be burned in the fire of Gehenna.[viii][57]

10. Words from the mouth of a wise man are gracious, while the lips of a fool consume him; [13] the beginning of his talking is folly, and the end of it is wicked madness. [14] Yet the fool multiplies words. No man knows what will happen, and who can tell him what will come after him?

The words of a wise man found in the generation when punishment comes upon the world can pray to drive out the punishment and finds mercy with the LORD. The foolish man's lips are full of anger, and therefore everyone is destroyed. The beginning and end of the words of a fool are evil intrigues. Also, the words of the foolish are useless and he will not know what will happen to him at the end.[58]

---

[56] IBID.
[57] IBID.
[58] IBID.

11. The toil of a fool *so* wearies him that he does not *even* know how to go to a
city.

> The labor of a fool is foolishness, which will weary him. He does not learn
> how to get to a city where the sage is so that he can receive instruction to
> rid himself of his foolishness.[59]

12. Woe to you, O land, whose king is a lad and whose princes feast in the
morning.

> This verse is a reference to Jeroboam in the Northern Kingdom after the
> division of Israel. Jeroboam abolished the morning sacrifices of the people
> to the LORD.[60]

13. Blessed are you, O land, whose king is of nobility and whose princes eat at
the appropriate time-- for strength and not for drunkenness.

> Happy Israel will be when Hezekiah, son of Ahaz rules. He was a
> descendant of King David and was a man strong in the Torah and fulfiled
> all the commandments. He restored the morning sacrifice through strength
> and not through sloth.[61]

14. Through indolence the rafters sag, and through slackness the house leaks.

> Through sloth, in the matter of the Torah and commandments, a man
> becomes so poor that he has no children. Dispising, the commandments
> for a woman, is does not separate herself during her time of menstruation.

---

[59] IBID.
[60] IBID.
[61] IBID.

The result will be a constant state of menstruation in her house. This state would prevent her from having children.[62]

15. *Men* prepare a meal for enjoyment, and wine makes life merry, and money is the answer to everything.

   The enjoyment is the preparation of the meal to serve t the poor and hungry. Wine is prepared for the thirsty (pure wine was mixed with water before it was served). To these men, righteous money will be given so that they can take care of themselves and continue to feed and help the poor.

16. Furthermore, in your bedchamber do not curse a king, and in your sleeping rooms do not curse a rich man, for a bird of the heavens will carry the sound and the winged creature will make the matter known.

   It is not right to curse the king. The angel Raziel proclaims every day from heaven upon Mount Horeb, and a voice goes through the whole world, and Elijah, the High Priest, flying through the air of heaven like an angel with wings and declares matters that are done in secret to all the inhabitants of the earth.[63]

Culture Section

Discussion

In biblical times jars containing oil, honey, and ointments were not covered. Therefore, the jars were not secure, and flies or other insects could get into the jars. Contaminated jars of ointments were not able to be sold in the market.[64]

---

[62] IBID.

[63] IBID.

[64] Rocco A. Errico and George M. Lamsa, *Aramaic Light on Ezra through the Song of Solomon* (Smyma, GA: Noohra Foundation, 2010).

Thoughts

Most of Kohelet, except for the beginning of chapter three, is not used in the Christian church. Perhaps the reason for this is that the church fathers were confused by Solomon's saying, for example, those sayings in chapter three. Without the Targum which offers explanations, it would be difficult to fully understand these proverbs.

Chapter Eleven

New American Standard 1995	Hebrew
[1] Cast your bread on the surface of the waters, for you will find it after many days. [2] Divide your portion to seven, or even to eight, for you do not know what misfortune may occur on the earth. [3] If the clouds are full, they pour out rain upon the earth; and whether a tree falls toward the south or toward the north, wherever the tree falls, there it lies. [4] He who watches the wind will not sow and he who looks at the clouds will not reap. [5] Just as you do not know the path of the wind and how bones *are formed* in the womb of the pregnant woman, so you do not know the activity of God who makes all things. [6] Sow your seed in the morning and do not be idle in the evening, for you do not know whether morning or evening sowing will succeed, or whether both of them alike will be good. [7] The light is pleasant, and *it is* good for the eyes to see the sun. [8] Indeed, if a man should live many years, let him rejoice in them all, and let him remember the days of darkness, for they will be many. Everything that is to come *will be* futility. [9] Rejoice, young man, during your childhood, and let your heart be pleasant during the days of young manhood. And follow the impulses of your heart and the desires of your eyes. Yet know that God	שְׁלַ֤ח לַחְמְךָ֙ עַל־פְּנֵ֣י הַמָּ֔יִם כִּֽי־בְרֹ֥ב הַיָּמִ֖ים תִּמְצָאֶֽנּוּ׃ [2] תֶּן־חֵ֥לֶק לְשִׁבְעָ֖ה וְגַ֣ם לִשְׁמוֹנָ֑ה כִּ֣י לֹ֥א תֵדַ֔ע מַה־יִּהְיֶ֥ה רָעָ֖ה עַל־הָאָֽרֶץ׃ [3] אִם־יִמָּלְא֨וּ הֶעָבִ֜ים גֶּ֗שֶׁם עַל־הָאָ֙רֶץ֙ יָרִ֔יקוּ וְאִם־יִפּ֥וֹל עֵ֛ץ בַּדָּר֖וֹם וְאִ֣ם בַּצָּפ֑וֹן מְק֛וֹם שֶׁיִּפּ֥וֹל הָעֵ֖ץ שָׁ֥ם יְהֽוּא׃ [4] שֹׁמֵ֥ר ר֖וּחַ לֹ֣א יִזְרָ֑ע וְרֹאֶ֥ה בֶעָבִ֖ים לֹ֥א יִקְצֽוֹר׃ [5] כַּאֲשֶׁ֨ר אֵֽינְךָ֤ יוֹדֵ֙עַ֙ מַה־דֶּ֣רֶךְ הָר֔וּחַ כַּעֲצָמִ֖ים בְּבֶ֣טֶן הַמְּלֵאָ֑ה כָּ֗כָה לֹ֤א תֵדַע֙ אֶת־מַעֲשֵׂ֣ה הָֽאֱלֹהִ֔ים אֲשֶׁ֥ר יַעֲשֶׂ֖ה אֶת־הַכֹּֽל׃ [6] בַּבֹּ֙קֶר֙ זְרַ֣ע אֶת־זַרְעֶ֔ךָ וְלָעֶ֖רֶב אַל־תַּנַּ֣ח יָדֶ֑ךָ כִּ֠י אֵֽינְךָ֤ יוֹדֵ֙עַ֙ אֵ֣י זֶ֣ה יִכְשָׁ֔ר הֲזֶ֥ה אוֹ־זֶ֖ה וְאִם־שְׁנֵיהֶ֥ם כְּאֶחָ֖ד טוֹבִֽים׃ [7] וּמָת֖וֹק הָא֑וֹר וְט֥וֹב לַֽעֵינַ֖יִם לִרְא֥וֹת אֶת־הַשָּֽׁמֶשׁ׃ [8] כִּ֣י אִם־שָׁנִ֥ים הַרְבֵּ֛ה יִחְיֶ֥ה הָאָדָ֖ם בְּכֻלָּ֣ם יִשְׂמָ֑ח וְיִזְכֹּר֙ אֶת־יְמֵ֣י הַחֹ֔שֶׁךְ כִּֽי־הַרְבֵּ֥ה יִהְי֖וּ כָּל־שֶׁבָּ֥א הָֽבֶל׃ [9] שְׂמַ֧ח בָּח֣וּר בְּיַלְדוּתֶ֗יךָ וִֽיטִֽיבְךָ֤ לִבְּךָ֙ בִּימֵ֣י בְחוּרוֹתֶ֔ךָ וְהַלֵּךְ֙ בְּדַרְכֵ֣י לִבְּךָ֔ וּבְמַרְאֵ֖י עֵינֶ֑יךָ וְדָ֕ע כִּ֧י עַל־כָּל־אֵ֛לֶּה יְבִֽיאֲךָ֥ הָאֱלֹהִ֖ים בַּמִּשְׁפָּֽט׃ [10] וְהָסֵ֥ר כַּ֙עַס֙ מִלִּבֶּ֔ךָ וְהַעֲבֵ֥ר רָעָ֖ה מִבְּשָׂרֶ֑ךָ כִּֽי־הַיַּלְד֥וּת וְהַֽשַּׁחֲר֖וּת הָֽבֶל׃

<table>
<tr><td>

will bring you to judgment for all these things.

[10] So, remove grief and anger from your heart and put away pain from your body, because childhood and the prime of life are fleeting.

</td><td></td></tr>
</table>

Process of Discovery

Linguistics Section

Linguistic Structure

[1] Cast your bread on the surface of the waters, for you will find it after many days.

[2] Divide your portion to seven, or even to eight, for you do not know what misfortune may occur on the earth.

[3] If the clouds are full, they pour out rain upon the earth; and whether a tree falls toward the south or toward the north, wherever the tree falls, there it lies.

[4] He who watches the wind will not sow and he who looks at the clouds will not reap.

[5] Just as you do not know the path of the wind and how bones *are formed* in the womb of the pregnant woman, so you do not know the activity of God who makes all things.

[6] Sow your seed in the morning and do not be idle in the evening, for you do not know whether morning or evening sowing will succeed, or whether both of them alike will be good. [7] The light is pleasant, and *it is* good for the eyes to see the sun.

[8] Indeed, if a man should live many years, let him rejoice in them all, and let him remember the days of darkness, for they will be many. Everything that is to come *will be* futility.

[9] Rejoice, young man, during your childhood, and let your heart be pleasant during the days of young manhood. And follow the impulses of your heart and the desires of your eyes. Yet know that God will bring you to judgment for all these things.

[10] So, remove grief and anger from your heart and put away pain from your body, because childhood and the prime of life are fleeting.

Discussion

This chapter contains more proverbs.

The Proverbs of this chapter

1. Cast your bread on the surface of the waters, for you will find it after many days.

    One should extend one's bread to the poor who travel in ships. By doing so your reward will be found in the world to come.[65]

2. Divide your portion to seven, or even to eight, for you do not know what misfortune may occur on the earth.

    Give a portion of the seed of your field in the month of Tishri and do not refrain from sowing seeds in Marcheshwan (from the Targum, meaning the eighth month). For you do not know what evil may come upon the earth and whether the earlier or the later crops will survive.[66]

3. If the clouds are full, they pour out rain upon the earth; and whether a tree falls toward the south or toward the north, wherever the tree falls, there it lies.

    If the clouds are filled with rain, they pour out their water on the earth because of the acts of the righteous. If there are no righteous people on the planet, the rain falls on the sea or the desert so that the people will not benefit from it. The drought will result in a famine. A drought and famine

---

[65] Rocco A. Errico and George M. Lamsa, *Aramaic Light on Ezra through the Song of Solomon* (Smyma, GA: Noohra Foundation, 2010).
[66] IBID.

can occur if Heaven decrees that the king and his counselors fail in their rulership.[67]

4. He who watches the wind will not sow and he who looks at the clouds will not reap.

    A person who pays attention to sorcery and divination will never do good. A person who compares the constellations and the clouds of heaven will find that they will disappear and not return.[68]

5. Just as you do not know the path of the wind and how bones *are formed* in the womb of the pregnant woman, so you do not know the activity of God who makes all things.

    Humans do not know the ways of the LORD. The people at that time did not know how the breath of the spirit of life entered the body of a fetus in the womb and did not know the gender of the child until it is born. Humans are not supposed to understand the wisdom of the LORD and why the LORD does what He does.[69]

6. [6] Sow your seed in the morning and do not be idle in the evening, for you do not know whether morning or evening sowing will succeed, or whether both of them alike will be good. [7] The light is pleasant, and *it is* good for the eyes to see the sun.

    In a man's youth, he should marry and beget children in the time of his old age; he must not leave his wife because she cannot bear children. The light

---

of the Torah is sweet and pleasant for it illuminates dim eyes and always a person to see the glory of the face of the Shekinah.[70]

7. Indeed, if a man should live many years, let him rejoice in them all, and let him remember the days of darkness, for they will be many. Everything that is to come *will be* futility.

    A man will live many years if he is in constant study of the Torah. He should remember that death will eventually find him, so he should not sin.[71]

8. Rejoice, young man, during your childhood, and let your heart be pleasant during the days of young manhood. And follow the impulses of your heart and the desires of your eyes. Yet know that God will bring you to judgment for all these things.

    Rejoice when young, but make sure that you do not commit any sin before the LORD.[72]

9. So, remove grief and anger from your heart and put away pain from your body, because childhood and the prime of life are fleeting.

    Remember to remove anger from your heart because it can cause one to sin.

---

[70] IBID.
[71] IBID.
[72] IBID.

Culture Section

Questioning the passage

1. What does it mean to cast bread upon the water? (v. 1)

   When a person returns home and is on the last stage of the journey, he/she might throw some dry loaves of bread he/she was carrying into a stream or river, thinking that they will not need it. Later on in the journey, the person gets hungry and might find floating on the water the same loaves that had been thrown and then picks them up to eat them. Delays in travel were typical during the time of Solomon.[73]

Thoughts

This chapter is another collection of proverbs from Solomon.

[73] Rocco A. Errico and George M. Lamsa, *Aramaic Light on Ezra through the Song of Solomon* (Smyma, GA: Noohra Foundation, 2010).

Chapter Twelve

Language

New American Standard 1995	Hebrew
[1] Remember also your Creator in the days of your youth, before the evil days come and the years draw near when you will say, "I have no delight in them"; [2] before the sun and the light, the moon and the stars are darkened, and clouds return after the rain; [3] in the day that the watchmen of the house tremble, and mighty men stoop, the grinding ones stand idle because they are few, and those who look through windows grow dim; [4] and the doors on the street are shut as the sound of the grinding mill is low, and one will arise at the sound of the bird, and all the daughters of song will sing softly. [5] Furthermore, men are afraid of a high place and of terrors on the road; the almond tree blossoms, the grasshopper drags himself along, and the caperberry is ineffective. For man goes to his eternal home while mourners go about in the street. [6] *Remember Him* before the silver cord is broken and the golden bowl is crushed, the pitcher by the well is shattered and the wheel at the cistern is crushed; [7] then the dust will return to the earth as it was, and the spirit will return to God who gave it.	וּזְכֹר אֶת־בּוֹרְאֶיךָ בִּימֵי בְּחוּרֹתֶיךָ עַד אֲשֶׁר לֹא־יָבֹאוּ יְמֵי הָרָעָה וְהִגִּיעוּ שָׁנִים אֲשֶׁר תֹּאמַר אֵין־לִי בָהֶם חֵפֶץ: [2] עַד אֲשֶׁר לֹא־תֶחְשַׁךְ הַשֶּׁמֶשׁ וְהָאוֹר וְהַיָּרֵחַ וְהַכּוֹכָבִים וְשָׁבוּ הֶעָבִים אַחַר הַגָּשֶׁם: [3] בַּיּוֹם שֶׁיָּזֻעוּ שֹׁמְרֵי הַבַּיִת וְהִתְעַוְּתוּ אַנְשֵׁי הֶחָיִל וּבָטְלוּ הַטֹּחֲנוֹת כִּי מִעֵטוּ וְחָשְׁכוּ הָרֹאוֹת בָּאֲרֻבּוֹת: [4] וְסֻגְּרוּ דְלָתַיִם בַּשּׁוּק בִּשְׁפַל קוֹל הַטַּחֲנָה וְיָקוּם לְקוֹל הַצִּפּוֹר וְיִשַּׁחוּ כָּל־בְּנוֹת הַשִּׁיר: [5] גַּם מִגָּבֹהַּ יִרָאוּ וְחַתְחַתִּים בַּדֶּרֶךְ וְיָנֵאץ הַשָּׁקֵד וְיִסְתַּבֵּל הֶחָגָב וְתָפֵר הָאֲבִיּוֹנָה כִּי־הֹלֵךְ הָאָדָם אֶל־בֵּית עוֹלָמוֹ וְסָבְבוּ בַשּׁוּק הַסֹּפְדִים: [6] עַד אֲשֶׁר לֹא־(יִרחק) [יֵרָתֵק] חֶבֶל הַכֶּסֶף וְתָרֻץ גֻּלַּת הַזָּהָב וְתִשָּׁבֶר כַּד עַל־הַמַּבּוּעַ וְנָרֹץ הַגַּלְגַּל אֶל־הַבּוֹר: [7] וְיָשֹׁב הֶעָפָר עַל־הָאָרֶץ כְּשֶׁהָיָה וְהָרוּחַ תָּשׁוּב אֶל־הָאֱלֹהִים אֲשֶׁר נְתָנָהּ: [8] הֲבֵל הֲבָלִים אָמַר הַקּוֹהֶלֶת הַכֹּל הָבֶל: [9] וְיֹתֵר שֶׁהָיָה קֹהֶלֶת חָכָם עוֹד לִמַּד־דַּעַת אֶת־הָעָם וְאִזֵּן וְחִקֵּר תִּקֵּן מְשָׁלִים הַרְבֵּה: [10] בִּקֵּשׁ קֹהֶלֶת לִמְצֹא דִּבְרֵי־חֵפֶץ וְכָתוּב יֹשֶׁר דִּבְרֵי אֱמֶת: [11] דִּבְרֵי חֲכָמִים כַּדָּרְבֹנוֹת וּכְמַשְׂמְרוֹת נְטוּעִים בַּעֲלֵי אֲסֻפּוֹת נִתְּנוּ מֵרֹעֶה אֶחָד: [12] וְיֹתֵר מֵהֵמָּה בְּנִי הִזָּהֵר עֲשׂוֹת סְפָרִים הַרְבֵּה אֵין קֵץ וְלַהַג הַרְבֵּה יְגִעַת בָּשָׂר: [13] סוֹף דָּבָר הַכֹּל נִשְׁמָע אֶת־הָאֱלֹהִים יְרָא וְאֶת־מִצְוֹתָיו שְׁמוֹר כִּי־זֶה כָּל־הָאָדָם:

⁸ "Vanity of vanities," says the Preacher, "all is vanity!"

⁹ In addition to being a wise man, the Preacher also taught the people knowledge; and he pondered, searched out and arranged many proverbs.

¹⁰ The Preacher sought to find delightful words and to write words of truth correctly.

¹¹ The words of wise men are like goads, and masters of *these* collections are like well-driven nails; they are given by one Shepherd.

¹² But beyond this, my son, be warned: the writing of many books is endless, and excessive devotion *to books* is wearying to the body.

¹³ The conclusion, when all has been heard, *is*: fear God and keep His commandments, because this *applies to* every person.

¹⁴ For God will bring every act to judgment, everything which is hidden, whether it is good or evil.

¹⁴ כִּי אֶת־כָּל־מַעֲשֶׂה הָאֱלֹהִים יָבִא בְמִשְׁפָּט עַל כָּל־נֶעְלָם אִם־טוֹב וְאִם־רָע:

Process of Discovery

Linguistics Section

Linguistic Structure

[End times warning] [1] Remember also your Creator in the days of your youth, before the evil days come and the years draw near when you will say, "I have no delight in them"; [2] before the sun and the light, the moon and the stars are darkened, and clouds return after the rain; [3] in the day that the watchmen of the house tremble, and mighty men stoop, the grinding ones stand idle because they are few, and those who look through windows grow dim; [4] and the doors on the street are shut as the sound of the grinding mill is low, and one will arise at the sound of the bird, and all the daughters of song will sing softly.

[Statement about fear] [5] Furthermore, men are afraid of a high place and of terrors on the road; the almond tree blossoms, the grasshopper drags himself along, and the caperberry is ineffective. For man goes to his eternal home while mourners go about in the street.

[Proverb] [6] *Remember Him* before the silver cord is broken and the golden bowl is crushed, the pitcher by the well is shattered and the wheel at the cistern is crushed; [7] then the dust will return to the earth as it was, and the spirit will return to God who gave it.

[Conclusion to the writing] [8] "Vanity of vanities," says the Preacher, "all is vanity!" [9] In addition to being a wise man, the Preacher also taught the people knowledge; and he pondered, searched out and arranged many proverbs. [10] The Preacher sought to find delightful words and to write words of truth correctly. [11] The words of wise men are like goads, and masters of *these* collections are like well-driven nails; they are given by one Shepherd. [12] But beyond this, my son, be warned: the writing of many books is endless, and excessive devotion *to books* is wearying to the body. [13] The conclusion, when all has been heard, *is*: fear God and keep His commandments, because this *applies to* every person. [14] For God will bring every act to judgment, everything which is hidden, whether it is good or evil.

Discussion

This chapter concludes the writings of King Solomon in this book.

Questioning the Passage

1. What are verses three and four describing?

   Solomon is describing the human body using symbolism and for times in life.

Phrase	Symbolism
Watchmen of the house	legs
Mighty men	arms
Grinding one's	teeth
Look through the window	eyes
Doors	old age

   The sound of birds at night tends to wake up older adults. The family unit consisted of mature, young adults, and children. They lived together under one roof.[74]

2. What does an almond tree symbolize? (v. 5)

   The almond tree symbolizes a man's maturity and his ability to have children. An almond tree produces numerous blossoms, and a man is expected to create many children. The phrase "the almond tree shall blossom" means that a man will begin having many children.[75]

3. What do the "locust" and "fragrance" symbolize? (v. 5)

   Locust and fragrance symbolize children, grandchildren, and great-grandchildren. In the Near East, some men marry as boys at the age of nine

---

[74] Rocco A. Errico and George M. Lamsa, *Aramaic Light on Ezra through the Song of Solomon* (Smyma, GA: Noohra Foundation, 2010).

[75] IBID.

or ten. Many of these men live to be 120 years old. When they reach that age, their home is filled with children, grandchildren, and great-grandchildren.[76]

4. What does verse five mean?

The Targum offers a warning to men that a time may come that they will not be able to have sexual intercourse. In time a man will go to the grave and the angels whom exact judgment go about like scribes (or mourners) in the street to write the man's sentence.[77]

The understanding of an afterlife and judgment at death was in its infancy. Therefore it is understandable that during Solomon's time, the idea of angels judging humans was believed. The idea that the LORD created humans above the angels developed much closer to the time of Yeshua.

5. What does the proverb of verses six and seven mean?

The body is being described is when it is approaching death. It is likened to the malfunctioning machinery of a well: rope, wheel and pitcher. "The cord (spine) snaps; the skull shatters; the stomach breaks, and the body is smashed."[78]

---

[76] IBID.

[77] Martin McNamara et al., *The Aramaic Bible. tne Targums: The Targum of Job, the Targum of Proverbs, the Targum of Qohelet*, 1991.

[78] Nosson Scherman and Meir Zlotowitz, *The Book of Megillos: the Five Megillos: a New Translation with Overviews and Annotations Anthologized from the Classical Commentators* (Brooklyn, NY: Mesorah Publications, 1986).

6. What does the "goad" symbolize? (v. 11)

The Targum states that goads symbolize sages and wise men who are full of knowledge.[79]

Culture Section

Questioning the passage

1. What is verse two referring?

In this verse, "sun" symbolizes beauty, glory, and majesty. The stars and the moon denote fortune and success. In ancient days when a man's beauty fades and his glory passes away, it was said: "His sun has set and his stars have disappeared behind the horizon." This sentence means that the man has lost his good looks, his power, and his fortune. Clouds symbolize sorrows because they stop the sunlight from reaching the ground. In ancient days people believed that the stars had something to do with a man's rise and decline, his birth, strength, and fortune.[80]

Thoughts

The book concludes with a reminder that life is precious, and that children are a blessing from the LORD. One day each of us will fade and will return to the LORD. Follow the Laws and Commandments of the LORD which leads to an abundant life.

---

[79] Martin McNamara et al., *The Aramaic Bible. the Targums: The Targum of Job, the Targum of Proverbs, the Targum of Qohelet*, 1991.
[80] Rocco A. Errico and George M. Lamsa, *Aramaic Light on Ezra through the Song of Solomon* (Smyma, GA: Noohra Foundation, 2010).

Bibliography

al., Martin McNamara et. 1991. *The Aramaic Bible, the Targums: The Targum of Job, Proverbs and Qohelet.* Collegeville, MN: Liturgical Press.

n.d. *Burial Definition and Meaning - Bible Dictionary.* Accessed January 20, 2020. https://www.biblestudytools.com/dictionary/burial.

Davis, Anne Kimball. 2012. *The Synoptic Gospels.* Albuquerque, NM.

Lamsa, Rocco A. Errico and George M. 2010. *Aramaic Light on Ezra through the Song of Solomon.* Smyrna, GA: Noohra Foundation.

Murai, Hajime. n.d. *Literary Structure (Chiasm, Chiasmus) of Ecclesiastes.* Accessed January 18, 2020. http://www.bible.literarystructure.info/bible/21_Ecclesiastes_pericope_e.html #7.

1986. *Back to School.* Directed by Paper Clip Productions.

Zlotowitz, Nosson Scherman and Meir. 1986. *The Book of Megillos:the Five Megillos: a New translation with overviews and Annotations.* Brooklyn, NY: Mesorah Publications.

[i] "Ibn Ezra was likely born in or around 1093 in Tudela, at that time within the northern reaches of Muslim Spain. There he passed the first five decades of his life, apparently eking out his living as a poet. Like so many other Jews, he fled Spain in the face of the Almohade onslaughts of 1140. For the next three decades he wandered through Europe, spending time in Rome, Lucca, Rouen, London, and Béziers. Nearly all of the substantial body of writing that he left behind dates to this period. The names of a few of his students, correspondents, rivals, and patrons are known. We are rather well-informed about Ibn Ezra's relationship with Judah Halevi; their exchanges are very instructive for the history of Jewish philosophy, and we will return to them below. On the other hand, none of his disciples (who in any event do not seem to have been numerous) has clarified for us any of the "secrets" that Ibn Ezra is fond to refer to." Source: https://plato.stanford.edu/entries/ibn-ezra/

[ii] Rabbi Solomon ben Isaac (Shlomo Yitzhaki), known as Rashi (based on an acronym of his Hebrew initials), is one of the most influential Jewish commentators in history. He was born in Troyes, Champagne, in northern France, in 1040. At age 17, Rashi received an education in the yeshiva of Rabbi Yaakov ben Yakar in Worms, where the "Rashi Chapel" was built years after his death (this chapel was subsequently destroyed during the German occupation in World War II, and rebuilt in 1950). At age 25, he returned to Troyes, where he became a rabbi. Since rabbis were not yet paid officials at this point in time, Rashi also worked with his family in the local vineyards. In 1070, he founded a yeshiva where he taught many disciples, some of whom would also go on to become prominent Jewish scholars. In 1096, Rashi witnessed the massacre of friends and family members at the hands of Crusaders en route to the Holy Land. He died in 1105 in Troyes. Source: https://www.myjewishlearning.com/article/who-was-rashi/

iii "Kara Joseph (before c. 1060-70), Bible commentator from the north of France. His father, Simeon, was apparently also a scholar, but S.J. Rapoport's ascription to him of the authorship of *Yalkut Shimoni* has been shown by A. Epstein to be without foundation (see bibl.). Joseph studied under his paternal uncle, *Menahem b. Ḥelbo, and was also a student and colleague of Rashi. Rashi obviously knew Kara, who was about 25 years his junior, since he mentions him (cf. Rashi on Is. 10:24 and 64:3) and quotes some of his interpretations; at least in one case he states that Kara told him an explanation of Menaḥem b. Ḥelbo. Recent scholarship asserts that there is no evidence that Kara studied under Rashi. There is evidence that the latter occasionally accepted his biblical exegesis, and Samuel b. Meir calls Kara "our colleague" (Commentary on Gen. 37:13). Kara was the first to copy and edit Rashi's commentary. In the process he added his own remarks, some of which were approved by Rashi and many of them were integrated into the standard Rashi commentary. Some 100 such notes were compiled by A. *Berliner in his *Pletath Soferim*. Kara lived mainly in Troyes and for a period in Worms and is known to have taken part in theological discussions with Christians."
Source: https://www.jewishvirtuallibrary.org/kara-joseph

iv About the time when the Jews of Spain and Portugal suffered the great tragedy of being driven from their homes and beyond the borders of their lands, Jewish life in Italy took a turn for the better. In Spain, centuries of Jewish learning and culture came to an end; in Italy, Jews could still live and learn and write great books.

The family of the Sfornos had been well known in Italy for several generations. Many a great rabbi bore that name and was a faithful leader to his community. But the most famous of all the Sfornos was Rabbi Obadiah ben Yaakov.

Obadiah was born in Cesena, Italy. His father, Rabbi Yaakov (Jacob) Sforno, was a great scholar, and the boy's first teacher. Obadiah, while still very young, showed that he had a good head for the study of the Torah which he loved very much. At an early age, when other children were just beginning to study the Talmud, he astonished everyone with a wide knowledge of it. At the same time he began to study mathematics and philosophy, and to write his own commentaries on the TeNaCh." Source: https://www.chabad.org/library/article_cdo/aid/111930/jewish/Rabbi-Obadiah-Sforno.htm

[v] "Composed in (c.1455 - c.1495 CE). Akeidat Yitzchak, written by the Spanish rabbi Isaac ben Moses Arama (c. 1420 – 1494) , is a collection of philosophical sermons on the Torah. The book is composed of 105 "gates" with each gate containing a sermon. Each sermon discusses a philosophical idea that comes from the chosen texts and a commentary that tries to solve the problems in the text. Akeidat Yitzchak was first published in 1522 in Salonika." Source: https://www.sefaria.org/Akeidat_Yitzchak?lang=bi

[vi] "Moshe Alshich Hebrew: משה אלשיך, also spelled Alshech, (1508–1593), known as the *Alshich Hakadosh (the Holy)*, was a prominent rabbi, preacher, and biblical commentator in the latter part of the sixteenth century.

The Alshich was born in 1508 in the Ottoman Empire, and was the son of Hayyim Alshich. He later moved to Safed where he became a student of Rabbi Joseph Caro. His students included Rabbi Hayim Vital and Rabbi Yom Tov Tzahalon. He died in Safed in 1593." Source: https://en.wikipedia.org/wiki/Moshe_Alshich

---

[vii] "David Altshuler was an 18th century Biblical commentator. Originally from the Iberian penninsula, his wanderings led him to Eastern Europe, where he served as rabbi of Jaworów, Poland. His notes and writings on Tanach were assembled by his son, Yehiel Hillel, and published under the name Metzudot." Source: https://www.sefaria.org/person/David%20Altschuler

[viii] "Gehenna, also called Gehinnom, abode of the damned in the afterlife in Jewish and Christian eschatology (the doctrine of last things). Named in the New Testament in Greek form (from the Hebrew Ge Hinnom, meaning "valley of Hinnom"), Gehenna originally was a valley west and south of Jerusalem where children were burned as sacrifices to the Ammonite god Moloch. This practice was carried out by the Israelites during the reigns of King Solomon in the 10th century BC and King Manasseh in the 7th century BC and continued until the Babylonian Exile in the 6th century BC. Gehenna later was made a garbage centre to discourage a reintroduction of such sacrifices.

The imagery of the burning of humans supplied the concept of "hellfire" to Jewish and Christian eschatology. Mentioned several times in the New Testament (*e.g.,* Matthew, Mark, Luke, and James) as a place in which fire will destroy the wicked, it also is noted in the Talmud, a compendium of Jewish law, lore, and commentary, as a place of purification, after which one is released from further torture." Source: https://www.britannica.com/topic/Gehenna

www.ingramcontent.com/pod-product-compliance
Lightning Source LLC
Chambersburg PA
CBHW060603120726
48002CB00010B/2797